Why Jesus HAD To Be Crucified

Damien Connolly

DEDICATION

This book is dedicated to all those who struggle to understand
the meaning of Jesus' Crucifixion

CONTENTS

CHAPTER 1
MAN'S DESTINY

"God, infinitely perfect and blessed in himself, in a plan of sheer goodness freely created man to make him share in his own blessed life" (CCC 1).

"The eternal Father, by a free and hidden plan of His own wisdom and goodness, created the whole world. His plan was to raise men to a participation of the divine life" (Lumen Gentium 2).

"Constituted in a state of holiness, man was destined to be fully "divinized" by God in glory" (CCC 398).

"The first man was not only created good, but was also established in friendship with his Creator and in harmony with himself and with the creation around him, in a state that would be surpassed only by the glory of the new creation in Christ" (CCC 374).

"The Church, interpreting the symbolism of biblical language in an authentic way, in the light of the New Testament and Tradition, teaches that our first parents, Adam and Eve, were constituted in an original "state of holiness and justice" (CCC 375).

"By the radiance of this grace all dimensions of man's life were confirmed. As long as he remained in the divine intimacy, man would not have to suffer or die. The inner harmony of the human person, the harmony between man and woman, and finally the harmony between the first couple and all creation, comprised the state called "original justice" (CCC 376).

To "Share In His Own Blessed Life"

From all eternity God has been living in complete bliss, fully content and satisfied in Himself. Nothing can "make God happier." He is and always has been perfectly Self-fulfilled. Yet out of love, God "freely created man to make him share in His own blessed life" (CCC 1). This statement from the Catholic Catechism does not mean that God wanted mankind to merely exist alongside His presence. It means something much deeper! God desired humans to be incorporated into His Being so that we might experience *His* life and *His* happiness within *us*. The Constitution on the Church, *Lumen Gentium*, echoes this teaching when it states that God had a "hidden plan" to "raise men to a participation in the divine life" (LG 2). Essentially, there is no difference between "sharing in His own blessed life" (CCC 1) and coming to a "participation in the divine life." Either way, man was destined to be fully "divinized" by God in glory" (CCC 398).

Original Holiness And Justice

The first humans, Adam and Eve, were not immediately created into a divinized state—a state of total unity with God...participating in the divine life. They would however, be *granted* this level of unity at some stage in the future, presumably after passing the "test" (as the Catholic Catechism calls it) posed by the Tree of the Knowledge of Good and Evil (more on that later). Rather, as the Catechism teaches, God originally established mankind in a state of "Original Holiness and Justice," meaning Adam and

Eve experienced (a) harmony within themselves, between one another and with the rest of creation, and (b) a friendship or intimacy with God (CCC 376).

They maintained this "intimacy" and "friendship" with ease, because they were created with a natural inclination to lovingly obey God in all things. This innate inclination to be obedient to God was part of what it meant to be human. When creating Adam and Eve, it was as if God set their basic default setting to "obedient to God." This does not mean however, that God predestined them, or pre-programed them to be obedient. No! If He did that, Adam and Eve would be no different than a robot and all their obedient actions would have no value, meaning or merit. Rather, God created Adam and Eve with a natural inclination to be obedient to Him, but this inclination did not overpower their free will.

Man's Destiny Interrupted By Sin

God's plan "to make" mankind "share in His own blessed life" (CCC 1) became frustrated and sidetracked by the Original Sin, which:

(a) Threw universal justice, symbolized by what theologians call the "scales of justice" out of balance.

(b) Destroyed mankind's state of Original Holiness and Justice. This means (among other things) that the natural "friendship" and "intimacy" Adam and Eve had with God became shattered.

(c) Caused human nature to become a downgraded, "fallen" version of itself. This fallen version of human nature involved having an inclination to sin, which only exacerbated the rift between man and God.

Obviously, Adam and Eve's disobedience in the Garden of Eden caused a LOT to go wrong! Nevertheless, God never gave up on His original plan to "raise men to a participation of the divine life" (LG 2). In the upcoming pages, we will attempt to explain exactly why and how Jesus' Crucifixion was needed to (a) rebalance the scales of justice (b) restore man to a harmonious relationship with himself and others and (c) bring mankind to "share in God's own life."

PRAYER

Lord, thank you so much for making me. You made me out of pure love and destined me to be united to you. In the meantime, I have to struggle against my tendencies to sin. Help me to always seek after a relationship with you and to ignore any desire for disobedience that might arise within me. Amen!

Questions:
1. How does it make you feel to know that God created you to share in His life?
2. How does it make you feel to know that every time you sin, you are time-wasting, only creating an obstruction to deeper intimacy with God?
3. What is original holiness and justice?

CHAPTER 2
SUSTAINING MANKIND IN EXISTENCE

"God created mankind in his image; in the image of God he created them; male and female he created them" (Genesis 1:27).

"With creation, God does not abandon his creatures to themselves. He not only gives them being and existence, but also, and at every moment, upholds and sustains them in being, enables them to act and brings them to their final end" (CCC 301).

"Man is the summit of the creator's work, as the inspired account expresses by clearly distinguishing the creation of man from that of the other creatures" (CCC 343).

"Of all visible creatures only man is "able to know and love his creator". He is "the only creature on earth that god has willed for its own sake", and he alone is called to share, by knowledge and love, in God's own life. It was for this end that he was created, and this is the fundamental reason for his dignity..." (CCC 356).

"Justice is the moral virtue that consists in the constant and firm will to give their due to God and neighbor" (CCC 1807).

Man: The Summit Of Creation

The book of Genesis describes in symbolic language the creation of the entire universe as taking place over six consecutive days. At the end of each day God looked at His handiwork and "saw that it was good." Yet after creating mankind in His own "image and likeness" God "looked at everything he had made, and found it very good" (Genesis 1:31). By telling us these things, scripture is revealing that mankind is the crowning glory, or summit of God's creative acts.

Creation As An Undeserved Gift

Of course, humans did nothing to deserve being created, let alone being the summit of creation! How could they? Before they were created, they didn't exist, and someone who doesn't exist is certainly in no position to earn/deserve anything! The creation of Adam and Eve then, was an act of undeserved goodness on God's part.

Retaining The Right To Life Through Obedience

Adam and Eve did not have the right to be created, but after being created, they were *accorded* the right to life and they retained this right so long as they remained obedient to (a) the laws of God which He placed in their hearts and (b) God's explicit law forbidding them to eat from the Tree of the Knowledge of Good and Evil. So long as they were obedient to God, they would retain their right to life and ensure their continued happy existence.

Being Obedient Is Part Of Human Nature

Being obedient to God came easy to our first parents. This is because, as discussed earlier, God created Adam and Eve in a state of Original Holiness and Justice. Disobedience on the other hand, is contrary to human nature. When Adam and Eve disobeyed God, they were deliberately ignoring/denying their human nature with its innate preference for obedience and acted as non-humans.

PRAYER

Thank you Lord for my life! I know I did nothing to deserve being created. I desire to live a life that expresses gratitude for each moment. Please help me to always carry in my heart an appreciation for all that has been granted to me—the people who love me, the universe that surrounds me, my ultimate destiny (to be united to you) and indeed my every breath! Even when things are tough and life seems very difficult, may I always remember and be thankful for my precious life. Amen!

Questions:

1. Why was it easy for Adam and Eve to be obedient to God?
2. God didn't give Adam and Eve a list of commandments. How did they know what He expected of them?
3. How does it make you feel to know that as a human, you are "very good" in the eyes of God?
4. Many people in the world believe that there is no God. They believe that the whole universe (humans included) is the result of a freak cosmic accident known as the Big Bang. For them, the Big Bang means that humans were not planned by a loving Creator-God. What do you think of this?

CHAPTER 3
ORIGINAL JUSTICE

"God created everything for man, but man in turn was created to serve and love God and to offer all creation back to him" (CCC 358).

"The first man was not only created good, but was also established in friendship with his Creator and in harmony with himself and with the creation around him, in a state that would be surpassed only by the glory of the new creation in Christ" (CCC 374).

"The Church, interpreting the symbolism of biblical language in an authentic way, in the light of the New Testament and Tradition, teaches that our first parents, Adam and Eve, were constituted in an original "state of holiness and justice". This grace of original holiness was "to share in...divine life" (CCC 375).

"As long as he remained in the divine intimacy, man would not have to suffer or die. The inner harmony of the human person, the harmony between man and woman, and finally the harmony between the first couple and all creation, comprised the state called "original justice" (CCC 376).

"The first man was unimpaired and ordered in his whole being because he was free from the triple concupiscence that subjugates him to the pleasures of the senses, covetousness for earthly goods, and self-assertion, contrary to the dictates of reason" (CCC 377).

"The sign of man's familiarity with God is that God places him in the garden. There he lives "to till it and keep it". Work is not yet a burden, but rather the collaboration of man and woman with God in perfecting the visible creation" (CCC 378).

A God Of Justice

Christianity teaches that God is perfectly "just." Since justice is defined as "the virtue whereby we give ourselves and others what they deserve" we know that before humans were created, God was forever in eternity acting "justly" towards Himself, giving Himself what He deserved—love. By simply loving Himself, God was acting justly towards Himself. And after creating humans, God's acts of justice began to include giving them what *they* deserved—love. Of course, loving humanity implied sustaining them in existence moment by moment. They "deserved" to be kept alive (a) because of who/what they were in and of themselves—beings created in God's image and likeness—and (b) because of their obedience to God's laws.

Adam And Eve's Lives Of Original Justice

As we have already established, Adam and Eve's very *nature* inclined them to be obedient to God's laws—to act "justly." Of course, this couldn't be any other way, since Adam and Eve were created in the image and likeness of a perfectly "just" God. Being just, was simply part and parcel of being human; it was their "default setting." Giving themselves, each other, and God what they "deserved to receive" came naturally to them, just as it came naturally to God. As such, Adam and Eve lived in harmony with each other, with all of creation and with God. As we have already seen, Christian theologians refer to this state of being as "Original Holiness and Justice."

Original Justice In The Garden Of Eden

The book of Genesis teaches that after bringing all things into being, God "saw that it was very good." This implies that, at least for a period of time, Adam and Eve were living out their lives in the manner God had intended. That is, they were acting "justly" towards each other and God. So long as they did this, God would ensure their continued existence.

PRAYER

Thank you Lord for showing me that I am called to live a just life and that among other things, this means that I am called to love myself. Help me to love myself in all situations. Help me to accept my individuality, my physicality, my gifts, my talents. Help me to realize that by loving myself, I am imitating you. Amen!

Questions:
1. What is the theological virtue of justice?
2. How do we know that Adam and Eve must have been living obedient and just lives in the Garden of Eden, at least for a period of time?
3. What "default setting," so to speak, did God create Adam and Eve with?

CHAPTER 4
"THE" ORIGINAL SIN

"Sin is an offense against God: "Against you, you alone, have I sinned, and done that which is evil in your sight." Sin sets itself against God's love for us and turns our hearts away from it. Like the first sin, it is disobedience, a **revolt against God** *through the will to become "like gods," knowing and determining good and evil. Sin is thus "love of oneself even to contempt of God." In this proud self- exaltation, sin is diametrically opposed to the obedience of Jesus, which achieves our salvation" (CCC 1850).*

"Now the snake was the most cunning of all the wild animals that the LORD God had made. He asked the woman, "Did God really say, 'You shall not eat from any of the trees in the garden'?" The woman answered the snake: "We may eat of the fruit of the trees in the garden; it is only about the fruit of the tree in the middle of the garden that God said, 'You shall not eat it or even touch it, or else you will die.'" But the snake said to the woman: "You certainly will not die! God knows well that when you eat of it your eyes will be opened and you will be like gods, who know good and evil." The woman saw that the tree was good for food and pleasing to the eyes, and the tree was desirable for gaining wisdom. So she took some of its fruit and ate it; and she also gave some to her husband, who was with her, and he ate it. Then the eyes of both of them were opened, and they knew that they were naked; so they sewed fig leaves together and made loincloths for themselves. When they heard the sound of the LORD God walking about in the garden at the breezy time of the day, the man and his wife hid themselves from the LORD God among the trees of the garden. The LORD God then called to the man and asked him: Where are you? He answered, "I heard you in the garden; but I was afraid, because I was naked, so I hid." Then God asked: Who told you that you were naked? Have you eaten from the tree of which I had forbidden you to eat? The man replied, "The woman whom you put here with me—she gave me

fruit from the tree, so I ate it." The LORD God then asked the woman: What is this you have done? The woman answered, "The snake tricked me, so I ate it." Then the LORD God said to the snake: Because you have done this, cursed are you among all the animals, tame or wild; On your belly you shall crawl, and dust you shall eat the days of your life. I will put enmity between you and the woman, and between your offspring and hers; They will strike at your head, while you strike at their heel. To the woman he said: I will intensify your toil in childbearing; in pain you shall bring forth children. Yet your urge shall be for your husband, and he shall rule over you. To the man he said: Because you listened to your wife and ate from the tree about which I commanded you, You shall not eat from it, Cursed is the ground because of you! In toil you shall eat its yield all the days of your life. Thorns and thistles it shall bear for you, and you shall eat the grass of the field. By the sweat of your brow you shall eat bread, Until you return to the ground, from which you were taken; For you are dust, and to dust you shall return. The man gave his wife the name "Eve," because she was the mother of all the living. The LORD God made for the man and his wife garments of skin, with which he clothed them. Then the LORD God said: See! The man has become like one of us, knowing good and evil! Now, what if he also reaches out his hand to take fruit from the tree of life, and eats of it and lives forever? The LORD God therefore banished him from the garden of Eden, to till the ground from which he had been taken. He expelled the man, stationing the cherubim and the fiery revolving sword east of the garden of Eden, to guard the way to the tree of life" (Genesis 3).

The Original Sin

The Catholic Catechism teaches that Genesis 3 uses "figurative language" (CCC 390). For example, we read about the snake, the Tree of the Knowledge of Good and Evil, the Tree of Life, the fruit etc. The Catholic Church teaches that while figurative language is used in Genesis 3, one thing can be taken as fact: the first parents of the human race were tempted by Satan into freely committing an act of disobedience which had disastrous consequences not only for them, but for the entire human race down to the present day. What that sin was exactly, we do not know.

PRAYER

Dear Lord, I am truly sorry for the times when I acted against your will. I know now that when I sin, I am revolting not just against your commands, but against you. When I sin, I am in some strange way imitating the sin of our first parents, Adam and Eve who loved themselves more than you. Help me to despise all sin and to do my best to please you in all things. Fill my heart with the desire to achieve my ultimate destiny—to share in the divine nature—the way you want, not the way I see fit. Amen!

Questions:

1. What do you think the fruit of the Knowledge of Good and Evil represents?
2. What do you think Adam and Eve's desire to eat from the Tree of the Knowledge of Good and Evil represents?
3. What do you think of the temptation to "become like God's, knowing good from evil"?
4. Why do you think Adam and Eve were prevented from eating from the Tree of Life after they committed the Original Sin?

CHAPTER 5
FROM LUCIFER TO SATAN

"Behind the disobedient choice of our first parents lurks a seductive voice, opposed to God, which makes them fall into death **out of envy**. Scripture and the Church's Tradition see in this being a fallen angel, called "Satan" or the "devil". The Church teaches that Satan was at first a good angel, made by God: "The devil and the other demons were indeed created naturally good by God, but they became evil by their own doing" (CCC 391).

"Scripture speaks of a sin of these angels. This "fall" consists in the **free choice of these created spirits**, who radically and irrevocably rejected God and his reign. We find a reflection of that rebellion in the tempter's words to our first parents: "You will be like God." The devil "has sinned from the beginning"; he is "a liar and the father of lies" (CCC 392).

"Then war broke out in heaven; Michael and his angels battled against the dragon. The dragon and its angels fought back, but they did not prevail and there was no longer any place for them in heaven. The huge dragon, the ancient serpent, who is called the Devil and Satan, who deceived the whole world, was thrown down to earth, and its angels were thrown down with it" (Revelation 12:7-9).

"Blameless were you in your ways from the day you were created, Until evil was found in you. Your commerce was full of lawlessness, and you sinned. Therefore I banished you from the mountain of God; the cherub drove you out from among the fiery stones. Your heart had grown haughty because of **your beauty**; You corrupted your wisdom because of **your splendor**. I cast you to the ground, I made you a spectacle in the sight of kings. Because of the enormity of your guilt, and the perversity of your trade, you defiled your sanctuary. I brought fire out of you; it devoured you; I made you ashes on the ground in the eyes of all who see you. All the nations who knew you are appalled on account of you; You have become a horror, never to be again" (Ezekiel 28:15-19).

Fallen Angels

Before God ever made human beings, He created the angels. The most glorious of them all was Lucifer, the angel of light. Sometime after creating the angels, or perhaps before creating them, God decided to create an even higher form of being— humans. This higher form of being would be created in His image and likeness and as such would more closely reflect His divine nature. This meant that Lucifer would no longer be "top dog" in heaven. While the bible is silent about the specifics of the fall of Lucifer, one plausible theory is that when Lucifer became aware of God's plan, his pride got the best of him, causing him to rebel against God. He even convinced one third of the angelic host to join in his rebellion! In response, God cast these angels from His presence who from then on became known as "fallen angels." Lucifer himself became known as Satan, or the Devil.

To Kill Or Not To Kill

One plausible theory suggests that when Satan saw Adam and Eve—the first humans from which the entire human race would descend—he was filled with violent envy. These two beings resembled God more closely than he ever could. All he wanted (presumably) was to kill them. But if he killed them that would only result in their souls returning to God in heaven. So in his envy, he planned to get them to sin against God, for doing so would defile God's image and likeness which they bore within them.

CHAPTER 6
MAKING EVIL ATTRACTIVE

"Man, tempted by the devil, let his trust in his Creator die in his heart and, abusing his freedom, disobeyed God's command. This is what man's first sin consisted of. All subsequent sin would be disobedience toward God and lack of trust in his goodness" (CCC 397).

"In that sin man preferred himself to God and by that very act scorned him. He chose himself over and against God, against the requirements of his creaturely status and therefore against his own good. Constituted in a state of holiness, man was destined to be fully "divinized" by God in glory. Seduced by the devil, he wanted to "be like God", but "without God, before God, and not in accordance with God" (CCC 398).

"Scripture portrays the tragic consequences of this first disobedience. Adam and Eve immediately lose the grace of original holiness. They become afraid of the God of whom they have conceived a distorted image - that of a God jealous of his prerogatives" (CCC 399).

Satan's Plan

As we saw in a previous chapter, God was planning on raising mankind to participation in His own blessed life. Man was thus on the fast track to becoming divinized. Satan on the other hand, planned on getting Adam and Eve to rebel (sin) against God by seeking, as the Catechism puts it, "to be like God" but "without God, before God and not in accordance with God" (CCC 398).

The Notion That God Is Controlling

Taking on the form of a snake/serpent, Satan approached Eve. His central goal was to get her to think of God as a controlling deity bent on holding her back from achieving divinity, all because He didn't want to share that status with anyone else.

Using his cunning and deceitful intellect, he said to her: "Did God really say, 'You shall not eat from <u>any</u> of the trees in the garden'?" His words were carefully chosen. God had not, at any stage, said anything like that! Rather, God instructed Adam and Eve to eat from ALL of the trees in the Garden except for one— the Tree of the Knowledge of Good and Evil. Nevertheless, by asking "did God *really* say you can't eat from <u>any</u> of the trees in the garden?" the devil was subtly introducing to the mind of Eve the concept of an overly controlling God.

The idea that God would be overly controlling had never entered her mind before, nor had she ever met anyone who opened themselves to even *consider* the possibility—until now. Now she is conversing with the serpent, who seems to be quite comfortable with entertaining the possibility. And of course, the devil wanted her to feel comfortable considering the possibility too.

A Selfish Manipulative Liar

At first, Eve protested, saying (Gen 3:2-3):

> *We may eat of the fruit of the trees in the garden; it is only about the fruit of the tree in the middle of the garden that God said, 'You shall not eat it or even touch it, or else you will die.'*

However, the devil responded with the following words (Gen 3:5):

> You certainly will not die! God knows well that when you eat of it your eyes will be opened and you will be like gods, who know good and evil.

With these words, the devil abruptly accuses God of being a liar and explains to Eve the reason why He lied: He didn't want Eve to become like Him!

A million thoughts must have raced through her mind as she considered the implications. She must have been thinking, "why didn't God simply tell me I had the chance to become like Him?" Or, "why would God prevent me from achieving my full potential by becoming like Him?" The devil had Eve right where he wanted her—doubting God's goodness and desiring to "to be like God" but "without God, before God and not in accordance with God" (CCC 398). With just a few sentences, the devil insinuated into the mind of Eve the concept of an evil, selfish and manipulative God. God had lied to them about the Tree of the knowledge of Good and Evil because, ostensibly, He didn't want to share being God with anyone else. And so, the devil convinced Eve that God was, as the Catechism puts it, "jealous of His prerogatives" (CCC 399).

The possibility that God was actively holding Eve back from achieving her true potential must have totally bewitched her. It was a fifty-fifty chance. Either God was good and benevolent or He was a manipulative liar bent on preserving His position as the one true God. Unfortunately, Eve (and Adam) took the bait and as the Catholic Catechism puts it, they let their "trust" in their Creator "die" (CCC 397).

CHAPTER 7
ORIGINAL SIN

"The doctrine of original sin is, so to speak, the "reverse side" of the Good News that Jesus is the Savior of all men, that all need salvation and that salvation is offered to all through Christ. The Church, which has the mind of Christ, knows very well that we cannot tamper with the revelation of original sin without undermining the mystery of Christ" (CCC 389).

"Scripture portrays the tragic consequences of this first disobedience. Adam and Eve immediately lose the grace of original holiness. They become afraid of the God of whom they have conceived a distorted image – that of a God jealous of his prerogatives" (CCC 399).

"The harmony in which they had found themselves, thanks to original justice, is now destroyed: the control of the soul's spiritual faculties over the body is shattered; the union of man and woman becomes subject to tensions, their relations henceforth marked by lust and domination. Harmony with creation is broken: visible creation has become alien and hostile to man. Because of man, creation is now subject "to its bondage to decay". Finally, the consequence explicitly foretold for this disobedience will come true: man will "return to the ground", for out of it he was taken. Death makes its entrance into human history" (CCC 400).

"How did the sin of Adam become the sin of all his descendants? The whole human race is in Adam "as one body of one man". By this "unity of the human race" all men are implicated in Adam's sin, as all are implicated in Christ's justice. Still, the transmission of original sin is a mystery that we cannot fully understand. But we do know by Revelation that Adam had received original holiness and justice not for himself alone, but for all human nature. By yielding to the tempter, Adam and Eve committed a personal sin, but this sin affected the human nature that they would then transmit in a fallen state. It is a sin which

will be transmitted by propagation to all mankind, that is, by the transmission of a human nature deprived of original holiness and justice. And that is why original sin is called "sin" only in an analogical sense: it is a sin "contracted" and not "committed" – a state and not an act" (CCC 404).

"Therefore, just as through one person sin entered the world, and through sin, death, and thus **death came to all, inasmuch as all sinned**" (Romans 5:12).

"You were dead in your transgressions and sins in which you once lived following the age of this world, following the ruler of the power of the air, the spirit that is now at work in the disobedient. All of us once lived among them in the desires of our flesh, following the wishes of the flesh and the impulses, and **we were by nature children of wrath, like the rest**" (Ephesians 2:1-3).

"All men are implicated in Adam's sin, as St. Paul affirms: "By one man's disobedience many (that is, all men) were made sinners": "sin came into the world through one man and death through sin, and so death spread to all men because all men sinned." The Apostle contrasts the universality of sin and death with the universality of salvation in Christ. "Then as one man's trespass led to condemnation for all men, so one man's act of righteousness leads to acquittal and life for all men"
(CCC 402).

"How did the sin of Adam become the sin of all his descendants? **The whole human race is in Adam** "as one body of one man". By this "unity of the human race" all men are implicated in Adam's sin, as all are implicated in Christ's justice. Still, the transmission of original sin is a mystery that we cannot fully understand…Adam and Eve committed a personal sin, but this sin affected the human nature that they would then transmit in a fallen state. It is a sin which will be transmitted by propagation to all mankind, that is, by the transmission of a human nature deprived of original holiness and justice. And that is why **original sin is called "sin" only in an analogical sense**: it is a sin "contracted" and not "committed" – a state and not an act" (CCC 404).

"For just as **in Adam all die**, so too in Christ shall all be brought to life.." (1 Corinthians 15:22).

"Therefore, just as through one person sin entered the world, and through sin, death, and thus death came to all, inasmuch as all sinned" (Romans 5:12).

"You were dead in your transgressions and sins in which you once lived following the age of this world, following the ruler of the power of the air, the spirit that is now at work in the disobedient. All of us once lived among them in the desires of our flesh, following the wishes of the flesh and the impulses, and **we were by nature children of wrath, like the rest**" (Ephesians 2:1-3).

The Consequences

The consequences of Adam and Eve's sin were staggering:

1. The universal scales of justice (God's system of justice) was thrown off balance.
2. Immediate loss of intimacy and friendship with God
3. Immediate loss of the right to live justly in the presence of God
4. Women would have intensified pain in childbirth
5. Men would experience great hardship in bringing food from the earth
6. Physical deterioration and eventual death
7. A strong inclination towards further sin (known in Christian theology as concupiscence)

8. Disharmony among human beings
9. Disharmony between humans and the rest of creation
10. All humans after Adam and Eve would be born with a fallen human nature, spiritually separated from God.

Downgraded Human Nature: 0.5

By disobeying God, Adam and Eve acted in an un-human way and in so doing they caused their human nature to become a shadow of its former self...weak, defective and prone to further sin and eventual death. If human nature was created "1.0," it became downgraded to "0.5" after the Original Sin.

Original Sin And "The" Original Sin

It should be noted that Christianity uses a specific term—Original Sin—to refer to the fallen-*ness* of human nature. To say "I am a fallen human" is no different than saying "I have Original Sin." However, when we speak about the Original Sin (with the definite article) we are referring to Adam and Eve's *act of sinning*.

We Are All Created From A Fallen Nature

Christianity teaches that Adam and Eve's downgraded form of human nature is what the rest of humanity came from. Their fallen nature is the stuff from which we have all been made. The bible teaches that even though we were not yet created, the entire human race was mysteriously "in him" (Adam) when he committed the Original Sin (1 Cor 15:22). It is as if Adam contained billions of seeds within him (symbolizing all potential, future humans) such that when he sinned, not only did he corrupt his own human nature, but also corrupted all of those seeds he contained within him. And since humans could only be generated from the "stuff" of Adam, all future humans were doomed to experience the corrupting effects of Adam's sin. For this reason, Adam and Eve's sin is often referred to by Catholic theologians as the Fall *of mankind*. Because of the Original Sin every human since Adam and Eve has been conceived with "Original Sin"—a fundamentally flawed human nature.

Not Fully Human

True human nature however is not fallen. Rather, to be truly human is to live each day in perfect loving obedience to God. From the moment of our conception however, we inherit a fallen human nature, which means that until the day we die, our fallen predisposition will be towards disobedience. The sad truth is, none of us have *ever* known what it is like to be *fully* human; we have only ever experienced life from a fallen (disobedient) perspective.

"Good But Fallen"

Having Original Sin means that we have all been born spiritually separated from God (that is, as spiritual orphans). Nevertheless, the Catholic Church teaches that humans are still "basically good." This means that Original Sin has not *completely* corrupted human nature. The image and likeness of God is still within us, although it has become dimmed and obscured by sin. Though we will all sin, deep down, the desire for God is still present within each of us and we have the capacity to prevent ourselves from committing grave, deliberate sins.

PRAYER

Dear Lord, I am sorry that our first parents, Adam and Eve, disregarded Your command and committed the Original Sin and that ever since, all humans, myself included, have been living disobedient lives. I long for a world where all people live justly, giving you the love and obedience You rightfully deserve. Even though it's very difficult for me, I accept the consequences of Adam and Eve's sin. Now, please give me strength to combat my own fallen tendencies to sin against you. Help me, every day, to experience more and more what it means to be "fully human" and to love you with all my heart in all things. "My Lord and my God, take from me everything that distances me from you. My Lord and my God, give me everything that brings me closer to you. My Lord and my God, detach me from myself to give my all to you" (CCC 226). Amen!

Questions:
1. What is the difference between Original Sin and "the" Original Sin?
2. What does the Catechism mean when it says that Original Sin is contracted, not committed?
3. In your opinion, what are the 3 worst consequences of the Original Sin?
4. What do you think of the biblical statement that when we live sinful lives, we are "children of wrath"? How do you think this phrase should be understood?
5. Many people believe that the Catholic teaching about Original Sin is negative and causes people to feel guilt. Do you agree or disagree?

6. What do you think of the Catholic phrase "good but fallen"? Is it positive or negative? Please elaborate.

7. What do you think of the statement that we have never experienced what it is like to be fully human?

8. What does being "fully human" look like?

9. In Ephesians 2, St. Paul says that when we live lives of sin, we are following the ruler of the power of the air. Who is that? Do you think that people even realize that the spirit of the ruler of the power of the air is at work in them, as St. Paul says? What do you think of this?

CHAPTER 8
INUNDATED BY SIN

"After that first sin, the world is virtually inundated by sin" (CCC 401).

"Behold, I was born in guilt, in sin my mother conceived me" (Psalm 51:7).

"...the desires of the human heart are evil from youth..." (Genesis 8:21).

"The heart is more deceitful than all else and is desperately sick; who can understand it?" (Jeremiah 7:19).

"The Lord has looked down from heaven upon the sons of men, to see if there are any who understand, who seek after God. They have all turned aside; together they have become corrupt; there is no one who does good, not even one" (Psalms 14:2-3).

All people who are not in Christ are *"sons of disobedience"* (Ephesians 2:2).

We are all *"by nature children of wrath"* (Ephesians 2:3).

Original Sin As Seen Throughout The Bible

The great tragedy of having Original Sin is that humanity is ever-destined, or doomed, to commit sin until the end of time. Humanity's penchant for sin is of course reflected throughout the scriptures: Adam and Eve's son Cain killed his brother Abel. A few generations later we read that Lamech killed a boy. And by the time we get to Noah (the tenth generation) we read that:

The LORD saw how great the wickedness of the human race had become on the earth, and that every inclination of the thoughts of the human heart was only evil all the time (Gen 6:5).

Even after the Great Flood, sin continued. Noah's son Ham committed such a great sin against him that he cursed his son Canaan. Abraham sinned, Isaac sinned, Esau sinned, Jacob sinned, Judah sinned…etc. etc. Even the greatest men of the bible like Moses (murder), David (adultery and manslaughter), Solomon (idolatry) were not immune to sin. As King David himself confessed, "All have turned away, all have become corrupt; there is no one who does good, not even one" (Ps 14:13). Similarly, in the New Testament, St. Paul writes that "all have sinned and fall short of the glory of God" (Rom 3:23).

PRAYER

Dear Lord, you have been patient with the whole human race ever since the beginning. Because you know all things, you must have known that Adam and Eve would sin and that the rest of the human race would all continue in the same manner. It must be difficult to watch us continually make the wrong choices. Help me come to terms with the fact that I am a sinner. Help me to learn the same lesson that St. Paul did—that I cannot save myself, but must rely on you completely. Amen!

Questions:

1. Research: Who are the only two exceptions to St. Paul's statement that "all have sinned and fallen short of the Glory of God"? Research your answer.

2. The bible states that by the tenth generation, "every inclination of the thoughts of the human heart was only evil all the time." This seems very, very stark. Do you think it's possible for us to have "evil" thoughts, but not realize it because we think that they are actually good? Discuss in a few sentences.

3. How does it make you feel to know that even the best people of the bible sinned, and sometimes greatly?

CHAPTER 9
THE SCALES OF JUSTICE

"Love the LORD, your God, therefore, and keep his charge, statutes, ordinances, and commandments always" (Deuteronomy 11:1).

"Blessed those who do what is right, whose deeds are always just" (Psalm 106:3).

"How can I repay the LORD for all the great good done for me?" (Psalm 116:12).

"For the LORD is a God of justice: happy are all who wait for him!" (Isaiah 30:18).

"You have been told, O mortal, what is good, and what the LORD requires of you: Only to do justice and to love goodness, and to walk humbly with your God" (Micah 6:8).

"There was a scholar of the law who stood up to test him and said, "Teacher, what must I do to inherit eternal life?" Jesus said to him, "What is written in the law? How do you read it?" He said in reply, "You shall love the Lord, your God, with all your heart, with all your being, with all your strength, and with all your mind, and your neighbor as yourself." He replied to him, "You have answered correctly; do this and you will live" (Luke 10:25-28).

"For this is love, that we walk according to his commandments; this is the commandment, as you heard from the beginning, in which you should walk" (2 John 1:6).

A Balanced Scale

The term "scales of justice" is used by theologians to symbolize humanity's status or standing before God. On one end of the scale, one finds God's love towards humanity, while on the other one finds humanity's loving obedience towards God. When the scales are evenly balanced, humanity can be said to be in a just relationship with God and the universe is said to be in balance. But when the scales are unbalanced through sin, the imbalance indicates that humanity has stopped treating God justly and that the universe is consequently out of balance.

The Debt Of Obedience

So long as God wasn't receiving perfect loving human obedience, the scales of justice remained out of balance. On one end of the scale, God was extending love and life to humanity while on the other, humanity continued to use this existence to indulge their sinful inclinations. And so, with each passing day, humanity became more and more indebted to God. Justice became "past due." And even if a human managed to live one day of perfect obedience—which was impossible anyway—that obedience would work to satisfy the requirements of that day only and would not compensate for the disobedience of former or future days. And so it went...with each passing day humanity continued to sin, and in so doing, racked up an enormous debt of obedience, a debt which was impossible to pay.

It might be helpful to think of perfect loving human obedience as a form of currency that is owed to God—because He deserves it—each and every day. After the Fall, mankind became spiritually bankrupt, unable to meet its payments.

PRAYER

My God, you have put up with so much! Mankind has, over and over again, insulted your honor and disrespected You by our sins. Ever since Adam and Eve's Original Sin there hasn't been a single day when you received the loving obedience you deserve. This is so sad! You have done so much for us! You even created the entire universe for us and destined us to participate in your own blessed life! Humanity owes you so much! But none of us can ever give You even one day's worth of what you deserve—perfect loving obedience! Everything we enjoy depends on your mercy. Thank you God. Amen!

Activity:

1. If perfect loving human obedience were an actual physical currency, what would it look like? Draw your 1 P.L.O. bill in full color.

CHAPTER 10
GOD STILL DESERVES OBEDIENCE

"Man's sins, following on original sin, are punishable by death" (CCC 602).

"I am the vine, you are the branches. Whoever remains in me and I in him will bear much fruit, because without me you can do nothing" (John 15:5).

"Do not be deceived, my beloved brothers: all good giving and every perfect gift is from above, coming down from the Father of lights, with whom there is no alteration or shadow caused by change" (James 1:17).

The Inability To Give God His Due

Adam and Eve's initial perfect and loving obedience towards God was not just something God desired—it was something He *deserved*. However, because of the fallen nature their sin produced, with its attendant predilection towards further sin, Adam and Eve plunged humanity into the disastrous predicament of *never* being able to render to its Creator the perfect loving obedience He so deserved to receive.

Each and every moment of each and every day, God *deserved* to receive perfect loving obedience from Adam and Eve, and for a brief time in the Garden of Eden, they did just that. It was normal and natural for them. Of course, Adam and Eve had been created in a state of Original Justice with a natural proclivity to perfect obedience. In the beginning then, rendering perfect loving obedience to God was *normal, realistic and attainable* and in no way outlandish. When Original Sin entered the picture however, perfect human obedience became an impossible and unrealistic goal.

Humanity Without The Right To Life

By withholding their perfect loving obedience from God, Adam and Eve ceased to act justly towards Him. They abused the very breath He had given them only to rebel against His good image which they bore within them. By so doing, they lost the *right* to live, and from that point on, God had the right to take their lives from them, at any moment. Indeed, every (fallen) human would eventually find him/herself in the exact same dilemma—unable to act justly towards their Creator and consequently unable to maintain their right to life.

God Still Deserves Perfect Loving Obedience

Of course, God knew that fallen humanity would be unable to deliver the level of perfect obedience He deserved to receive. But this by no means indicates that God no longer deserved to receive it. The Original Sin affected human nature only. God was still God and He *still deserved* to receive perfect loving human obedience. And so long as He was not receiving it the universal scales of justice remained out of balance.

PRAYER

Most loving God, you deserve all my love and heartfelt obedience. Because of my willful sins I know I have no right to live in your presence. But now, I want to live out the rest of my life in a way that pleases you. It would be right and just to give You what You deserve. I am thankful for your mercy and am happy to do my very best each day. Fill me Lord with eyes to see You everywhere and with a heart full of love for everyone I see. Amen!

Questions:

1. What impact does sin have of our right to live in the presence of God?
2. How does it make you feel to know that when you sin willfully, you are abusing the very breath that God gave to you?
3. What do you think of the fact that God sees all of your actions, even your thoughts and all the motivations of you heart?
4. How does it make you feel to know that because of your willful sins you have lost the right to live?
5. Shouldn't every breath be a celebration, a praise of our Creator?

CHAPTER 11
WHY CONTINUE HUMAN EXISTENCE?

> *"Man's sins, following on original sin, are punishable by death"* (CCC 602).
>
> *"No creature is concealed from him, but everything is naked and exposed to the eyes of him to whom we must render an account"* (Hebrews 4:13).
>
> *"But do not ignore this one fact, beloved, that with the Lord one day is like a thousand years and a thousand years like one day. The Lord does not delay his promise, as some regard "delay," but he is patient with you, not wishing that any should perish but that all should come to repentance"* (2 Peter 3:8-9).

Was God Turning A Blind Eye To Sin?

The fact that God was extending existence to humanity despite its complete unworthiness raises a very important question: "Was God turning a blind eye to sin, and if He was, doesn't this show that God was turning a blind eye to justice itself?" The answer of course is "no!"

1. God Understood Mankind's Bankruptcy

For starters, God knew and understood well that Adam and Eve and the rest of fallen humanity were in a state of utter moral and spiritual bankruptcy and that it was therefore impossible for them to render the perfect loving obedience He deserved.

2. God's Love For Humanity

Of course, the other option—hypothetically speaking—was to terminate all human life. As we have seen, Adam and Eve lost the right to live in the presence of God and God reserved the right to discontinue their existence at any point thereafter. But His love for humanity prevented Him from taking this course of action.

3. Injustice Would Remain

Besides being contrary to the love of God, discontinuing human existence wouldn't solve the underlying problem of an out of balance scales of universal justice. If God simply terminated human existence He would be like a debt collector who, never getting paid, decides to end the lives of those indebted to Him. The source of the problem (disobedient humans) would disappear, but the problem itself—unpaid debt—would remain. God would remain "out of pocket," uncompensated, dishonored and insulted.

4. God Set A Plan Of Salvation In Motion

Recognizing that fallen humans were completely unable to live even a single day of perfect loving obedience and not wanting the scales of justice to remain out of balance forever, God, motivated by a true love for humanity, was content to set into motion a plan of salvation which would eventually (a) balance the scales of justice and (b) enable humanity to continue to render to Him, until the end of time, the perfect loving human obedience He deserves to receive. His plan of salvation (discussed in the following chapter) was set into motion immediately after the Original Sin.

Of course, God knew it would take time—thousands of years in fact—for all the pieces of His plan to come together. Nevertheless, His patience is not to be confused with indifference towards justice. The fact that His plan was set in motion from the very beginning shows that God was actively concerned about correcting the problem of universal injustice.

PRAYER

Thank you Lord for your great love for us. Even though we sinned and caused universal justice to go out of balance, you never abandoned us. You never gave up on your original plan to make us participate in your own blessed life. You set into motion a plan that would not only make up for our sins, but which would heal our fallen nature. Amen!

Questions:

1. If God terminated human existence just because humans did not deserve to be alive, what would that solve?
2. Does God expect perfect loving obedience from fallen humans?

CHAPTER 12
GOD'S PLAN OF SALVATION

"Then the LORD God said to the snake: Because you have done this, cursed are you among all the animals, tame or wild; On your belly you shall crawl, and dust you shall eat all the days of your life. I will put enmity between you and the woman, and between your offspring and hers; They will strike at your head, while you strike at their heel" (Genesis 3:14-15).

*"This passage in Genesis is called the Protoevangelium ("first Gospel"): the first announcement of the Messiah and Redeemer, of **a battle between the serpent and the Woman, and of the final victory of a descendant of hers**" (CCC 410).*

*"The Christian tradition sees in this passage an announcement of the **"New Adam"** who, because he "became obedient unto death, even death on a cross", makes amends superabundantly for the disobedience, of Adam. Furthermore many Fathers and Doctors of the Church have seen the woman announced in the Protoevangelium as Mary, the mother of Christ, the **"new Eve""** (CCC 411).*

"By the grace of God Mary remained free of every personal sin her whole life long" (CCC 493).

*"The Virgin Mary "cooperated through free faith and obedience in human salvation" (LG 56). She uttered her yes "in the name of all human nature" (St. Thomas Aquinas, STh III, 30, 1). By her obedience she became **the new Eve**, mother of the living" (CCC 511).*

*"Jesus is the new Adam who... (is) totally obedient to the divine will. In this, Jesus is the devil's conqueror... Jesus' victory over the tempter in the desert anticipates victory at **the Passion, the***

supreme act of obedience of his filial love for the Father" (CCC 539).

"In this proud self- exaltation, sin is diametrically opposed to the obedience of Jesus, which achieves our salvation" (CCC 1850).

"In conclusion, just as through one transgression condemnation came upon all, so through one righteous act acquittal and life came to all. For just as through the disobedience of one person the many were made sinners, so through the obedience of one the many will be made righteous" (Romans 5:18-19).

"By his obedience unto death, Jesus accomplished the substitution of the suffering servant, who "makes himself an offering for sin", when "he bore the sin of many", and who "shall make many to be accounted righteous", for "he shall bear their iniquities" (ccc 615).

God's Plan

In simple terms God's plan was to be born as a human (Jesus) and to live a life of perfect human obedience. He would also demonstrate intense and extreme obedience by dying for the truth about His own identity as God and King of the Jews (more on that later). The plan was for His one life of perfect human obedience—especially His intense obedience as demonstrated on the Cross—to counterbalance all of the acts of disobedience (sins) ever committed by humans, including the Original Sin. As the Catechism confirms, "Jesus substitutes his obedience for our disobedience" (CCC heading) and it is "the obedience of Jesus, which achieves our salvation" (CCC 1850).

The *Proto-Evangelium*

Right after Adam and Eve sinned God announced to the devil in cryptic/prophetic language His plan of salvation. This plan, outlined in Genesis 3:14-15 is

J
referred to by Christians as the *Proto-Evangelium*, meaning the "first Gospel." It is the "Good News" (Gospel) in a nutshell. His plan entailed putting "enmity" between (a) the snake and its offspring, and (b) "the woman" and her offspring. Christian tradition holds that the snake and its offspring is a reference to the devil and all who are in deliberate rebellion against God, while the "woman" and her "offspring" is a direct reference to Mary and her Son, Jesus. It is as if God was saying to the devil, "you may have succeeded in turning Adam and Eve against Me, but you'll never defeat Mary and Jesus."

It should come as no surprise therefore that the Catholic Church frequently refers to Jesus as the "New Adam" and to Mary as the "New Eve." Together, Mary and Jesus were destined to "strike" at the devil's head, while the devil and his followers would "strike" at "their heel." This striking at one another is of course, a reference to the all-out spiritual battle God was planning between the devil and his minions on one side, and Jesus and Mary on the other. More specifically, Christian tradition believes that this striking is an allusion to the Crucifixion, which would result in the physical death of Jesus.

The Immaculate Conception

The Catholic Church teaches that when Mary was conceived in the womb of her mother St. Ann, she did not contract Original Sin. In other words, God prevented Original Sin from entering into Mary from the moment she was conceived. The term "Immaculate Conception" refers to the event where God preserved Mary's human nature from contracting Original Sin at the moment of her conception. Since Mary's human nature had no sin, the state of existence she experienced was the same as (if not better than) the state that Adam and Eve experienced *before* they committed the Original Sin. The Catholic Church celebrates the Immaculate Conception on December 8. It is a "holy day of obligation," meaning all Catholics must go to Mass on that day.

Mother Of God

Of course, the Catholic Church also teaches that Mary never committed any actual sins after her conception! She could have sinned, but unlike Eve, she didn't. Because Mary had no sin from the moment of her conception through her youth, she merited to become the Mother for God. By calling Mary the "Mother of God," the Catholic Church is not suggesting that she gave Jesus His divine nature. Mary gave Jesus his *human nature* only, but since Jesus is God, it is indeed correct to refer to her as the "Mother of God."

"Fruit Of Thy Womb"

The first woman (Eve) helped Adam to commit disobedience by giving him some kind of "fruit." Similarly, the "New Eve" (Mary) helped the "New Adam" (Jesus) to defeat the devil by giving Him some kind of "fruit." The "fruit" Mary gave to Jesus was His human nature—particularly His human body. Without this human nature, Jesus would have been completely unable to live a life of *human* obedience. And since it was Jesus' life of human obedience that saves humanity, we can conclude that Mary played a key role in reversing the effects of Adam and Eve's sin and in redeeming mankind. In the very beginning, it was Eve who initiated the first act of disobedience and in the New Testament, it is Mary who initiated the ultimate act of human obedience (by giving a human body to Jesus). *Together* then, Mary and Jesus strike at the head of the devil and his followers.

When Mary became pregnant with Jesus she went to visit her cousin Elizabeth, who was already six months pregnant with a boy who would later become John the Baptist. As she approached her cousin, Elizabeth exclaimed, "blessed is the fruit of thy womb"! By using these specific words, the writer of the bible is trying to get us, the readers, to make the connection...that Mary is the New Eve.

PRAYER
Dear Lord, thank you so much for planning to become human and to live a life of perfect obedience to make up for my sins, which included dying in order to demonstrate intense obedience to God the Father. I am amazed when I think of the lengths to which you were willing to go, just to make up for my sins. Thank you for loving me! I want to live the rest of my life in gratitude for all you have done for me. Amen!

Questions:

1. When did God announce His plan to save humanity?
2. Who did God announce His plan to?
3. What is the *Proto-Evangelium*?
4. Make a list of the various titles the Catholic Church uses to refer to Mary.
5. What fruit did Mary give to Jesus?
6. Why do we call Mary the Mother of God?
7. When we call Mary the Mother of God, what are we not trying to imply?
8. What did Jesus do with the fruit he received?
9. Why was it necessary for Jesus to become human?
10. Explain what is meant by the Immaculate Conception
11. On what date is the Immaculate Conception celebrated?

CHAPTER 13
BECOMING A *REAL* HUMAN

> "The word became flesh to make us "partakers of the divine nature": "for this is why the word became man, and the son of god became the son of man: so that man, by entering into communion with the word and thus receiving divine sonship, might become a son of God." "For the son of god became man so that we might become God." "The only-begotten Son of God, wanting to make us sharers in his divinity, assumed our nature, so that He, made man, might make men gods" (CCC 460).
>
> "The unique and altogether singular event of the incarnation of the son of God does not mean that Jesus Christ is part God and part man, nor does it imply that he is the result of a confused mixture of the divine and the human. He became truly man while remaining truly God. Jesus Christ is true God and true man" (CCC 464).

The Hypostatic Union
Of course, God wasn't planning on giving up His divine nature in order to become human! Rather, His plan to "become" human simply involved "taking on" an additional nature—the human nature. God therefore would have two natures. Jesus was 100% divine and 100% human *at the same time*. The union of both natures in the divine Person of Jesus is referred to by the Catholic Church as the "hypostatic union."

Fully United Yet Fully Distinct
The Catholic Church teaches that Jesus' human and divine natures became *fully* united in such a mysterious way that His divinity did not become negatively affected or watered down by His humanity. Similarly, His humanity did not become

overwhelmed, enhanced, aided or boosted by His divinity. Rather, as the Catholic Church puts it, both natures, though fully united, remained completely "distinct" from one another. With both natures kept "distinct" from one another, Jesus was able, at any point, to operate from either a divine or human perspective.

Human Nature V. Any Other Nature

Of course, God could have taken on ANY nature—that of a dog, or a cat, or an angel etc. And He could have lived a life of perfect dog obedience, or cat obedience or angelic obedience. But living a perfectly obedient life as an animal or even as an angel would never serve to counterbalance *human* disobedience. To counterbalance *human* <u>dis</u>obedience, He would need to live a life of *human* <u>o</u>bedience, and to do that He would need a true human nature!

The Integrity Of Jesus' Humanity

It's important to remember that only a life of perfect human obedience could make up for human disobedience. As such, it was absolutely necessary for God to take on a real/true human nature and to make sure this human nature remained pure. This is precisely why both natures were kept "distinct" from one another. If they weren't "distinct" from one another, His human nature would end up being positively affected by His divinity and this would only result in a fake, souped-up version of a human nature; and a boosted, souped-up, enhanced human nature is really not a human nature at all.

No, God needed a REAL human nature to live a REAL human life and He preserved the purity/integrity of His humanity by keeping it distinct from His divinity.

So long as both natures remained "distinct" from one another, He would be able to live a real/true human life of obedience and consequently, counterbalance human disobedience.

PRAYER
My God, I am blown away when I remember that you took absolutely no short-cuts when it came to saving us. Even though your divinity was not affected by the human nature you took on, you didn't use your divine nature as a shield to protect you from human sorrow, pain and suffering. Thank you God for everything you have done for me. Amen!

Questions:
1. Why didn't God take on the nature of a dog or a tree or an angel?
2. What is the hypostatic union?
3. Why was it necessary for Jesus' two natures to be kept distinct from one another?
4. Why was it necessary for God to experience life from the perspective of a human nature?
5. Why could God not use His divine nature to shield Him from human suffering?

CHAPTER 14
ANIMAL SACRIFICE:
FORESHADOWING THE CRUCIFIXION

> *"Since the law has only a shadow of the good things to come, and not the very image of them, it can never make perfect those who come to worship by the same sacrifices that they offer continually each year. Otherwise, would not the sacrifices have ceased to be offered, since the worshipers, once cleansed, would no longer have had any consciousness of sins? But in those sacrifices there is only a yearly remembrance of sins, for it is impossible that the blood of bulls and goats take away sins. For this reason, when he came into the world, he said: "sacrifice and offering you did not desire, but a body you prepared for me; holocausts and sin offerings you took no delight in" (Hebrews 10:1-6).*

God Reveals His Plan Slowly

God knew what He had to do to counterbalance the sins of the world:

(a) Become human
(b) Live a life of perfect loving human obedience
(c) Offer His death to God the Father as the most intense expression of His human obedience

However, He never explicitly revealed these plans to anyone. Rather, throughout the bible, His plan of salvation remained somewhat of a mystery. Over many hundreds of years, through prophecies (like the *Proto-Evangelium*) and other hidden messages and events recorded in the bible, God slowly revealed to mankind His intentions.

The Theme Of Animal Sacrifices Introduced

The bible teaches that after Adam and Eve sinned they became aware of their nakedness and created clothes for themselves by sewing fig leaves together. Later, God created His own clothing line for them from leather. Question is, where did this leather come from? God, or Adam, or Eve, must have killed an animal to procure the material. Experts agree that here we have the first reference to animal sacrifices in the bible. Many believe that this detail is recorded to teach us that in order to "cover over" sin, something must first die. Animal sacrifices were thus used by God to reveal to mankind His intentions of one day dying for the sins of humanity.

God Will Provide Himself

About two thousand years before the birth of Jesus, God promised a man named Abraham that He would make a "great nation" out of him. Jesus was to be born into this great nation. Abraham's second son Isaac (not his first born Ishmael) was chosen by God to continue building His great nation. One day however, when Isaac was in his teenage years, God asked Abraham to sacrifice him on Mt. Moriah. Even though doing so would seemingly wipe out any chances of a future "great nation" Abraham complied with God's request and began to make preparations.

While Isaac carried the wood for the sacrifice he asked his father, "Here are the fire and the wood, but where is the sheep for the burnt offering?" Abraham replied, "God will provide Himself the lamb." Of course the "lamb" was supposed to be Isaac, but it's also possible Abraham was hoping God might change His mind and ask Abraham to sacrifice a real lamb instead. Nevertheless, Abraham couldn't have chosen his words more wisely. Spoken two thousand years before the birth of Jesus, he uttered a profound prophecy—that someday, God *will* "provide Himself" as a sacrificial "lamb" for humanity. Incidentally, by carrying the wood up Mt. Moriah, Isaac was foreshadowing Christ Himself, who carried the Cross up Mt. Calvary.

The First Passover

Roughly five hundred years after Abraham, the descendants of Isaac had become a "nation" of 1.5 - 2 million people. Problem was, they were all enslaved in the land of Egypt. God however, told Moses to speak to Pharaoh and ask him to "let My people go." Moses warned Pharaoh that if he didn't comply, God would cause terrible plagues to fall on Egypt. But Pharaoh was stubborn and wouldn't give in. As a result, God caused the promised plagues to come upon Egypt—the Nile turned to blood, frogs took over the land, gnats swarmed the air, pestilence took over the land, hailstones destroyed plants and animals, the sun became darkened for three days etc. The only way Pharaoh could stop the plagues was to ask Moses for mercy. But after Moses discontinued each plague, Pharaoh reverted to his stubbornness and refused to let the Hebrews go.

Freedom came eventually, after the tenth and final plague—the death of the firstborn sons. Moses explained to the Hebrew slaves that God's angel of death would kill ALL the first born sons in Egypt. He then gave them instructions to ensure that their own firstborn sons would not be affected...

The Hebrews were to do the following:

(a) Kill a lamb
(b) Make sure to not break any of the lamb's bones
(c) Smear the lamb's blood around the entrance to their homes
(d) Cook the lamb
(e) Eat the lamb
(f) Burn the remains of the lamb

As promised, the angel of death took the lives of all the firstborn sons in Egypt except for the firstborn Hebrew baby boys. When the angel saw the blood of the lamb around the entranceway, he "passed over" that (Hebrew) house and spared the lives of those firstborn sons inside. By requiring the death of a lamb in order to spare the lives of the Hebrews, God was teaching His people that for a life to be spared another life must be given up.

Of course, the Passover Lamb is a symbol of Jesus. He was killed, none of His bones were broken, His blood is applied to our homes (our bodies) when we receive the Eucharist, His flesh is eaten at every Mass, and as the smoke from the burned sacrifice rises into the air, so too Jesus rose from the dead.

An Elaborate Sacrificial System
After escaping from Egypt, Moses brought the Hebrews to Mt. Sinai. There they received very detailed and specific instructions for a sacrificial system unlike any the world has ever known. Specific sins called for specific animals and their blood had to be sprinkled in specific locations according to a specific order. Nothing could be out of place. Sacrifices were to be carried out with

meticulous attention to detail. Every day, morning and evening, the Jews were required to sacrifice to God. Besides these routine/daily sacrifices, the Jews were expected to offer additional sacrifices for individual sins. Only "perfect" animals—animals with no defects—were accepted. Defective or diseased animals were categorically rejected. The Jews had to give their best.

A Bloodthirsty God?

Readers of the bible are often turned off when they read about the elaborate and demanding sacrificial system God required the Jews to perform. But that's because most people automatically associate animal sacrifices with pagan sacrifices. The capricious pagan gods of lore craved the blood of animals and humans alike and withheld favors from their devotees until their quotas were met. Pagan sacrifices were offered simply to placate a fickle god into extending worldly favors.

The God of the bible however, was nothing like the pagan gods. There was nothing about death itself, or blood itself, that pleased Him. As the bible states, "Sacrifice and offering you did not desire...holocausts and sin offerings you took no delight in" (Hebrews 10:5-6). For the biblical God, animal sacrifices were necessary because of what they symbolized.

What Did Animal Sacrifices Symbolize?

1. **OUR OWN DEATH AND OUR AWARENESS THAT WE DESERVE TO DIE:** The life of the animal was offered to God as a symbolic substitute for the life of the sinner. As already discussed, when we sin we forfeit our right to

life. By offering to God the life of an animal, the sinner is symbolically showing God that he understands he no longer deserves to live. But rather than kill himself (which would be immoral) the sinner would offer the life of his best animal instead. This was done in the hopes that God would regard the animal's death as a symbolic substitute for the death of the sinner.

2. **PERFECT LOVING OBEDIENCE:** Sin is disobedience. God however, deserves to receive perfect loving obedience from all humans. When a person sins, it is only fitting that he should offer God some gesture of obedience in an effort to offset his disobedience. The death of the animal was used for such a purpose. This is because the animal "obediently" went along with the entire process that ended in its death. The animal would never run away, never flinch, never complain. Rather, the animal would simply follow the priest as it was led to the slaughter. Of course, the animal had no awareness of what was going on; so it wasn't being "obedient" in the true sense of the term. Nevertheless, the animal's placid cooperation with the priest was used to symbolically represent, and replace, the disobedience in the life of the sinner.

Activity:

1. Draw and color in a comic strip depicting everything the Hebrews had to do to ensure the Angel of Death would "pass over" them.
2. Write God's diary. In it, He explains exactly why He desires sacrifice.

CHAPTER 15
MESSIANIC PROPHECIES OF ISAIAH

Introduction To The Prophet Isaiah

The Prophet Isaiah lived in the Southern Kingdom of Judea in the 700s B.C. At that time sin was rampant throughout the *entire* land (the Southern Kingdom of Judea *and* Northern Kingdom of Israel). Isaiah warned both kingdoms to stop sinning! His message to the northerners was that God was about to let the Assyrian Empire destroy them as punishment for their Covenant breaking. Unfortunately, they didn't listen. In 722 B.C. the Assyrian army arrived and did exactly as Isaiah predicted. The northern kingdom (known as "Israel") was conquered and the Israelites who lived there were taken as captives and scattered all over the Assyrian Empire, never to return again. This event is known as the *diaspora* (dispersion). The ten northern tribes became known as the "ten lost tribes of Israel."

Isaiah also gave his own southern kingdom plenty of advance notice about the coming Babylonian attack (which would take place in 586 B.C.). He warned that if they didn't stop breaking God's commands they too would be conquered and exiled from the land. But just like with the northern kingdom, the Southern Jews didn't listen and in the end, they were conquered and exiled by the Babylonians, just as Isaiah predicted. But unlike the Northern Israelites who were scattered all over Assyria never to return, the Southern Jews were made captives in the city of Babylon and returned to their land, seventy years later.

The Southern Jews were allowed to return to their land because after the Babylonian Empire itself was conquered by the Persian Empire; and when the Persian King Cyrus learned that many Jews were living in Babylon, he graciously granted them permission to return to their land of origin. He even allowed them to have a Jewish King, rebuild their Temple (which the Babylonians destroyed) and worship according to their own religion. The one caveat was that the Jews had to remain his subjects. In other words, the Jews got to return home, install a king and rebuild their Temple, but they had to go on paying taxes to Cyrus and continue obeying Persian laws. The Jewish King therefore was merely a puppet. His job was to rule the Jews *for* the Persian Empire according to Persian law.

The Jews, though grateful to Cyrus for the ability to return to the land, restore their Temple and call themselves a "kingdom," wanted something more— total political independence. They wanted to break free from the Persian Empire completely and live according to their own Jewish Law (the Laws of Moses contained in the Torah). But everybody knew the Persians would NEVER grant them full political independence. That kind of freedom had to be won...by warfare.

The Southern Jewish Kingdom was a tiny blip on the radar screen compared to the massive Persian Empire. There was absolutely no way the Jews could successfully wage war against them and force them out of their land. Nevertheless, the Jews never gave up hope that someday God would send them a mighty, miracle working, warrior-king who would do just that. They referred to this person as their "Messiah" (meaning anointed). So, besides constantly warning his people about how God was going to exile them, Isaiah also comforted his audience with prophecies concerning the future Messiah. Though Isaiah was not the only prophet to describe a savior figure, his descriptions of the Messiah are numerous and colorful. We will now take a look at some of his depictions.

Activity:
Record on video, a 2-3 minute monologue from the perspective of Isaiah discussing (a) what happened to the Northern Kingdom (b) what will happen to the Southern Kingdom and (c) what to expect from the Messiah.

#1.   Messiah Will Bring About World Peace

"In days to come, The mountain of the LORD's house shall be established as the highest mountain and raised above the hills. All nations shall stream toward it. Many peoples shall come and say: "Come, let us go up to the LORD's mountain, to the house of the God of Jacob, That he may instruct us in his ways, and we may walk in his paths." For from Zion shall go forth instruction, and the word of the LORD from Jerusalem. He shall judge between the nations, and set terms for many peoples. They shall beat their swords into plowshares and their spears into pruning hooks; One nation shall not raise the sword against another, nor shall they train for war again" (Isaiah 2:2-4).

In this passage Isaiah depicts a beautiful scene set sometime in the distant future. In his vision, he observes all nations coming to the Lord's house in Jerusalem in order to learn from Him. He also predicts that the Lord will "judge between the nations and set terms for many peoples." This mysterious figure seems to be ruling over the whole world as an Emperor! The end result of His rule? World peace!

#2   Messiah Will Be Born Of A Virgin

> *"Therefore the Lord himself will give you a sign; the young woman, pregnant and about to bear a son, shall name him Emmanuel" (Isaiah 7:14).*

The literal meaning of Emmanuel is "God is with us." The Gospel of Matthew interprets the words "young woman" as "virgin." For Christians then, this passage serves as a prophecy about the virgin birth of Jesus, who receives the title (not the name) Emmanuel:

> All this took place to fulfill what the Lord had said through the prophet: "Behold, the virgin shall be with child and bear a son, and they shall name him Emmanuel," which means "God is with us (Matthew 1:22-23).

3   Messiah Is God/Father/King Forever

"For a child is born to us, a son is given to us; upon his shoulder dominion rests. They name him Wonder-Counselor, God-Hero, Father-Forever, Prince of Peace. His dominion is vast and forever peaceful, Upon David's throne, and over his kingdom, which he confirms and sustains by judgment and justice, both now and forever. The zeal of the LORD of hosts will do this!" (Isaiah 9:5-6).

In this passage, Isaiah is believed to be describing the young Messiah as a boy who,

(a) Rules on King David's throne (as Messiah)
(b) Rules over a "vast" domain (presumably not limited to Israel)
(c) Rules this dominion with justice "forever" (which indicates the Messiah will somehow live forever)
(d) Is called "God"
(e) Is called "Father-Forever"

#4   Messiah Will Be A Miracle Worker

"Say to the fearful of heart: Be strong, do not fear! Here is your God, he comes with vindication; With divine recompense he comes to save you. Then the eyes of the blind shall see, and the ears of the deaf be opened; Then the lame shall leap like a stag, and the mute tongue sing for joy. For waters will burst forth in the wilderness, and streams in the Arabah" (Isaiah 35:4-6).

Here Isaiah tells his Jewish audience that God will save and vindicate them by punishing their enemies (presumably Assyria and Babylon). On a more spiritual level, Isaiah was speaking of how God would save them from the powers of sin and darkness. The prophet mentions that when this saving occurs, the blind, the deaf, the lame and the mute will be miraculously cured.

In the Gospel of Luke, St. John the Baptist (Jesus' second cousin) sent some of his followers to ask Jesus whether or not He was the awaited Messiah. In His reply, Jesus linked His work with Isaiah's prophecy:

> When the men came to him, they said, "John the Baptist has sent us to you to ask, 'Are you the one who is to come, or should we look for another?'" At that time he cured many of their diseases, sufferings, and evil spirits; he also granted sight to many who were blind. And he said to them in reply, "Go and tell John what you have seen and heard: the blind regain their sight, the lame walk, lepers are cleansed, the deaf hear, the dead are raised, the poor have the good news proclaimed to them. And blessed is the one who takes no offense at me (Luke 7:20-23).

CHAPTER 16
THE SERVANT OF THE LORD

> *"For as by one man's disobedience many were made sinners, so by one man's obedience many will be made righteous."* By his obedience unto death, Jesus accomplished the substitution of the suffering Servant, who *"makes himself an offering for sin"*, when *"he bore the sin of many"*, and who *"shall make many to be accounted righteous"*, for *"he shall bear their iniquities"*. Jesus atoned for our faults and made satisfaction for our sins to the Father" (CCC 615).

Who Is The Servant Of The Lord?

Perhaps more than anything, Isaiah is best known for his cryptic and obscure descriptions of a mysterious figure who he calls the Servant of the Lord. These descriptions are contained in a cluster of passages known as the Servant Songs (Chapters 42:1-9, 49:1-7, 50:4-11, 52:13-53:12). Oddly enough, these songs seem to describe two completely different people—a powerful, miracle working Davidic King who will rule the world from Jerusalem, and a lowly servant who is killed for the sins of the people. Of course, Christians believe that *all* of Isaiah's descriptions point to Jesus, who paradoxically *was* both a Davidic King and a Suffering Servant.

Servant Song 1 - Isaiah 42:1-9

"Here is my servant whom I uphold, my chosen one with whom I am pleased. Upon him I have put my spirit; he shall bring forth justice to the nations. He will not cry out, nor shout, nor make his voice heard in the street. A bruised reed he will not break, and a dimly burning wick he will not quench. He will faithfully bring forth justice. He will not grow dim or be bruised until he establishes justice on the earth; the coastlands will wait for his teaching. Thus says God, the LORD, who created the heavens and stretched them out, who spread out the earth and its produce, Who gives breath to its people and spirit to those who walk on it: I, the LORD, have called you for justice, I have grasped you by the hand; I formed you, and set you as a covenant for the people, a light for the nations, To open the eyes of the blind, to bring out prisoners from confinement, and from the dungeon, those who live in darkness. I am the LORD, LORD is my name; my glory I give to no other, nor my praise to idols. See, the earlier things have come to pass, new ones I now declare; Before they spring forth I announce them to you"

Characteristics:
1. The Servant delights God the Father.
2. The Spirit of the Father is upon him.
3. The Servant will bring "justice to the nations," which seems to indicate that he will have great influence over other governments.
4. He will not "cry out, nor shout, nor make his voice heard in the street" (v. 2). This indicates that the Servant will not be seeking attention, or running a political campaign. Rather, the Servant will do his work quietly.

5. The Servant will not break a bruised reed or snuff out a smoldering wick (v 3). These seem to be metaphors describing people who carry a lot of hurt, pain and sorrow (perhaps self-inflicted through sin). Isaiah is saying that the Servant will know how to respond to certain sinners with gentleness.

6. The Servant will be a covenant for "the people" (meaning, the Jewish people).

7. The Servant will be a "light for the nations" indicating that he will also be a great role model for the Gentiles.

8. The Servant will release captives from prison (no doubt Isaiah has spiritual captivity in mind).

Servant Song 2 - Isaiah 49:1-7

"Hear me, coastlands, listen, distant peoples. Before birth the LORD called me, from my mother's womb he gave me my name. 2He made my mouth like a sharp-edged sword, concealed me, shielded by his hand. He made me a sharpened arrow, in his quiver he hid me. 3He said to me, You are my servant, in you, Israel, I show my glory. 4Though I thought I had toiled in vain, for nothing and for naught spent my strength, Yet my right is with the LORD, my recompense is with my God. 5For now the LORD has spoken who formed me as his servant from the womb, That Jacob may be brought back to him and Israel gathered to him; I am honored in the sight of the LORD, and my God is now my strength! 6It is too little, he says, for you to be my servant, to raise up the tribes of Jacob, and restore the survivors of Israel; I will make you a light to the nations, that my salvation may reach to the ends of the earth. 7Thus says the LORD, the redeemer, the Holy One of Israel, To the one despised, abhorred by the nations, the slave of rulers: When kings see you, they shall stand up, and princes shall bow down Because of the LORD who is faithful, the Holy One of Israel who has chosen you"

Characteristics:

1. The Servant will be called to do God's work before being born and will receive his name from God before his birth – Is 49:1
2. The Servant will have a way with words; He will be able to cut down his enemies with his speech – Is 49:2
3. The Servant will be like an arrow hidden in the quiver of God (His secret weapon). This indicates that he will not be noticed by his enemies for a period of time but will eventually be used openly – Is 49:2

4. The Servant is referred to by God as "Israel." This leads Jewish interpreters to conclude that the Servant of the Lord must be the nation of Israel. Christians disagree and maintain that the Servant of the Lord can be referred to as Israel because Jesus had 12 apostles and can therefore be compared to Abraham's grandson Jacob (later known as Israel) who had 12 sons. Additionally, Jesus is the originator of the spiritual kingdom of God (the Church) as Jacob/Israel was the patriarch of the nation of Israel – Is 49:3

5. The Servant will think to himself *"I had toiled in vain, for nothing and for naught spent my strength..."* This indicates that the Servant will, at least at some stage, be made to feel like he has worked all his life for nothing – Is 49:4

6. The Servant's main purpose is "That Jacob may be brought back to him and Israel gathered to him." This means that his job is to direct all Israelites back to God. Incidentally, Christians point out that since the Servant's job is to direct "Israel" back to God, he himself can hardly be the nation of Israel – Is 49:5

7. The Servant's other purpose is to be a "light to the Gentiles" in order that salvation may reach the entire globe – Is 49:6

8. The Servant will be "despised and abhorred by the nations" (i.e., Gentiles). In Jesus' lifetime He was hated by the Gentiles in the form of the Romans who crucified Him – Is 49:7

9. The Servant will be bowed down to by Kings and other world leaders – Is 49:7

10. The Servant will "restore the land" – Is 49:8

Servant Song 3 - Isaiah 50:4-11

"The Lord GOD has given me a well-trained tongue, That I might know how to answer the weary a word that will waken them. Morning after morning he wakens my ear to hear as disciples do; 5The Lord GOD opened my ear; I did not refuse, did not turn away. 6I gave my back to those who beat me, my cheeks to those who tore out my beard; My face I did not hide from insults and spitting. 7The Lord GOD is my help, therefore I am not disgraced; Therefore I have set my face like flint, knowing that I shall not be put to shame. 8He who declares my innocence is near. Who will oppose me? Let us appear together. Who will dispute my right? Let them confront me. 9See, the Lord GOD is my help; who will declare me guilty? See, they will all wear out like a garment, consumed by moths. 10Who among you fears the LORD, heeds his servant's voice? Whoever walk in darkness, without any light, Yet trust in the name of the LORD and rely upon their God! 11All you who kindle flames and set flares alight, Walk by the light of your own fire and by the flares you have burnt! This is your fate from my hand: you shall lie down in a place of torment"

Characteristics:

1. The Servant will know how to lift up the weary with his speech – Is 50:4
2. The Servant does "not refuse" or "turn away" from God. This shows that he will be sinless and un-rebellious towards God – Is 50:5
3. The Servant will give his back to those who beat him...his cheeks to those who tear out his beard. This is a vivid description of what happened to Jesus during His Passion—He was beaten and mocked – Is 50:6

4. Even though He will be beaten, He is confident ("flint faced") that God will prove his innocence – Is 50:7

5. The Servant will not be afraid to face those who accuse him of sin. He states "let them confront me" – Is 50:8

6. The Servant believes that those who condemn him will come to nothing. They will "wear out like a garment, consumed by moths" – Is 50:9

7. The Servant believes that he himself will inflict torment on those who condemn him – Is 50:9

Servant Song 4 - Isaiah 52:13-53:12

"See, my servant shall prosper, he shall be raised high and greatly exalted. 14Even as many were amazed at him—so marred were his features, beyond that of mortals his appearance, beyond that of human beings—15So shall he startle many nations, kings shall stand speechless; For those who have not been told shall see, those who have not heard shall ponder it. Who would believe what we have heard? To whom has the arm of the LORD been revealed? 2He grew up like a sapling before him, like a shoot from the parched earth; He had no majestic bearing to catch our eye, no beauty to draw us to him. 3He was spurned and avoided by men, a man of suffering, knowing pain, Like one from whom you turn your face, spurned, and we held him in no esteem. 4Yet it was our pain that he bore, our sufferings he endured. We thought of him as stricken, struck down by God and afflicted, 5But he was pierced for our sins, crushed for our iniquity. He bore the punishment that makes us whole, by his wounds we were healed. 6We had all gone astray like sheep, all following our own way; But the LORD laid upon him the guilt of us all. 7Though harshly treated, he submitted and did not open his mouth; Like a lamb led to slaughter or a sheep silent before shearers, he did not open his mouth. 8Seized and condemned, he was taken away. Who would have thought any more of his destiny? For he was cut off from the land of the living, struck for the sins of his people. 9He was given a grave among the wicked, a burial place with evildoers, Though he had done no wrong, nor was deceit found in his mouth. 10But **it was the LORD's will to crush him with pain**. By making his life as a reparation offering, he shall see his offspring, shall lengthen his days, and the LORD's will shall be accomplished through him. 11Because of his anguish he shall see the light; because of his knowledge he shall be content; My servant, the just one, shall justify the many, their *iniquity he shall bear. 12Therefore I will give him his portion among the many, and he shall divide the spoils with the mighty, Because he surrendered himself to death, was counted among the transgressors, Bore the sins of many, and interceded for the transgressors."*

Characteristics:

1. The Servant "had no majestic bearing to catch our eye, no beauty to draw us to him..." This shows that he will look like a regular human - Is 53:3

2. The Servant will be "spurned and avoided by men." The reason for being spurned and avoided is because the people believe that the Servant is experiencing great suffering as a punishment from God for his sins – Is 53:3

3. The Servant will be "held in no esteem." Again, the reason being because the people are convinced he is guilty of great sin – Is 53:3

4. The Servant will take on our pain and our suffering. He will suffer for us – Is 53:4

5. The Servant will be considered punished by God – Is 53:4

6. The Servant will be pierced and crushed for our sins – Is 53:5

7. The Servant's wounds will bring healing to us – Is 53:5

8. The Servant will be killed like a lamb who doesn't fight back – Is 53:7

9. The Servant will be slaughtered while no one protests – Is 53:8

10. The Servant will be killed for the sin of those who put him to death (Isaiah says for the sin

of "my people" which must be a direct reference to his people, the Jews) – Is 53:8

11. The Servant's "life" will be a "reparation" or offering "for sin" (which was a specific kind of sacrifice to take away sin described in Leviticus 4) – Is 53:10

12. After the Servant suffers and makes his "life" an "offering for sin" (which necessarily involves being killed) he will somehow "see his offspring and prolong his days" and "see the light of life." This is an obvious reference to Jesus' resurrection. His "offspring" is a reference to all Christians – Is 53:11

Because The Prophets Foretold It?

When studying the prophets and prophetic events and procedures such as the Passover and the Jewish sacrificial system, it is important to avoid concluding that Jesus had to be Crucified simply "because the prophecy had to be fulfilled." The prophecies and prophetic deeds of the Old Testament did not cause what they foretold. While they certainly attest to the foreknowledge of God, they do not explain the theology behind why Jesus HAD to be Crucified.

PRAYER

Oh my God, I am astounded by the precision of Isaiah's prophecies. He could only have been talking about you, Jesus! He spoke about your suffering in such detail...seven hundred years before the fact. You had been planning to die in this gruesome way ever since the Original Sin and started to reveal your plan bit by bit over the millennia. Thank you God for giving me this clear and unmistakable series of prophecies. I understand that Jesus had to die to give you the most intense act of loving obedience, and not necessarily because it was foretold. These prophecies help to confirm and strengthen my faith. Amen!

Activity:

1. Create a collage of the characteristics of the Servant of the Lord. Be sure to add biblical references.

CHAPTER 17
A NARCISSISTIC GOD?

The Need To Receive Perfect Loving Obedience

As discussed in chapter 11, God's decision to let human life continue despite humanity's unworthiness cannot be taken as proof that He lacked concern for justice. Rather, as was shown, God's concern for universal justice was so great that He set into motion a plan of salvation which would ultimately rebalance the scales of justice. (He does this of course, while still allowing the possibility of eternal separation from Him for those who obstinately die in a state of mortal sin). His plan involved Jesus offering the most intense act of human obedience to God the Father—the Crucifixion.

Concern for justice is certainly a noble and praiseworthy attribute. Yet, when one considers the extreme nature of the Crucifixion, one might be tempted to ask, "was rebalancing the scales of justice THAT important?" Or, "Why couldn't God just let our sins slide for the sake of His Son?" Or, "Was God being selfish or needy or narcissistic by requiring Jesus to die just so He could heal His wounded pride and "get the obedience He deserved"? The answer to all of these questions of course, is "no"! It was categorically imperative that God rebalance the scales of justice for the following reasons:

1. God Could Not Deny Himself/His Nature

God's "just" nature required Him to act justly not only towards Adam and Eve, but also towards Himself. If God simply turned a blind eye to sin by ignoring the amount of obedience that was owed Him, that very action would demonstrate His indifference towards justice itself. And if God stopped caring or never cared about receiving His due from humanity, if God's mercy caused Him to simply ignore the sins of the human race and sweep them under His divine rug, He could be charged, logically, with inadvertently dishonoring *Himself* and acting unjustly towards *Himself!* But acting unjustly towards Himself would constitute denying His very nature, something the New Testament says God "cannot do" (2 Tim 2:13). For in denying Himself, He would cease to be God.

2. Preserving His Just Nature For Us

The Catholic Church teaches that God created humans so that we might "share in His own blessed life" (CCC 1). This does not mean that God wanted humans to enjoy His presence from a distance, as it were. Rather, God's plan for us to "share in His life" implies an intense participation in His very Being. This participation in God's divinity is brought about by uniting us to His Being, and any human who becomes united to Him will automatically come to have a share in all things related to His divinity, including His divine qualities/attributes. "The two shall become one."

If, hypothetically, it was possible for God to ignore justice and turn a blind eye to sin, He would thereby become unjust and could only offer humanity a participation in His unjust Being. In other words, if God became unjust by ignoring human sin, we, upon uniting ourselves to Him, would come to participate in a downgraded version of God. But by staying true to His essential nature as a "just God" and by requiring humanity to render to Him His just due, God preserves the integrity of His justice and offers us the chance to unite ourselves to, and absorb the qualities of a most perfect, holy and just God.

Therefore, while it may *seem* selfish of God to demand and require perfect loving human obedience from His Son in the form of the Crucifixion, He does this (a) to safeguard the integrity of His own Justice so that (b) mankind might have the opportunity of uniting to (and absorbing) a God of perfect Justice and not an unjust, push-over God. In sum, God's requirement that He should receive the obedience that was due to Him through the Crucifixion of His Son Jesus demonstrates His wisdom, His glory and His most amazing love, as ultimately, the true beneficiaries of his seeming "selfishness" are those who are baptized into Him. Praise be to God!

PRAYER

Forgive me dear Lord if I ever allowed myself to consider the possibility that you were selfish by requiring Jesus' death in order to uphold your honor. Now I see that you did it to safeguard your just nature so that ultimately we might be able to unite to a God of perfect justice and share in your perfection. Thank you so much Lord. Amen!

Questions:

1. What would happen to justice itself, or even to God if He just let humanity's sins slide?
2. Explain how demanding Jesus' death was an act of selflessness on the part of God the Father.

CHAPTER 18
SAVED BY JESUS' LIFE OR DEATH?

"This man, delivered up by the set plan and foreknowledge of God, you killed, using lawless men to crucify him" (Acts 2:23).

"For I handed on to you as of first importance what I also received: that Christ died for our sins in accordance with the scriptures" (1 Cor 15:3).

"In this is love: not that we have loved God, but that he loved us and sent his Son as expiation for our sins" (1 John 4:10).

"Then he says, "Behold, I come to do your will"... By this "will," we have been consecrated through the offering of the body of Jesus Christ once for all" (Hebrews 10:9–10).

"The next day he saw Jesus coming toward him and said, "Behold, the Lamb of God, who takes away the sin of the world" (John 1:29).

"For Christ also suffered [other translations: died] for sins once, the righteous for the sake of the unrighteous, that he might lead you to God" (1 Peter 3:18).

"The desire to embrace his Father's plan of redeeming love inspired Jesus' whole life, for his redemptive passion was the very reason for his Incarnation" (CCC 607).

"The Council of Trent emphasizes the unique character of Christ's sacrifice as "the source of eternal salvation" and teaches that "his most holy Passion on the wood of the cross merited justification for us." And the Church venerates his cross as she sings: "Hail, O Cross, our only hope" (CCC 617).

Why Was Jesus' Crucifixion Required By God?

So far, we have established that God the Father's plan was for Jesus to offer to Him a LIFE of perfect loving human obedience to counterbalance all the sins of mankind. This however, raises a very obvious question: If Jesus' LIFE of obedience is what was needed to balance the scales of justice, why then the need for His death, especially His death by Crucifixion?

Intense Obedience Was Needed

Since the beginning of the world, God had witnessed INTENSE, deliberate human disobedience. In order to counterbalance this INTENSE disobedience, an act of intense obedience had to be offered to God. Jesus' acts of human obedience as a child and as a carpenter however, were not intense enough to make up for the sins of mankind. This is mainly because His daily acts of obedience (being an obedient son to Mary and Joseph, obeying the Laws of Moses etc.) came naturally and effortlessly to Him and as such, they did not serve to demonstrate the extent of His obedience. Something more was needed. Namely, Jesus needed to be put into a situation where it would be very difficult for Him to be obedient. For, to be obedient when it is easy has some value, but to be obedient when it is difficult has immense worth in the eyes of God. The Crucifixion provided Jesus with a set of circumstances wherein it would be extremely difficult for Him to be obedient.

Treason And Blasphemy

When we examine the New Testament, it becomes clear that Jesus was put to death for two reasons:

1. Jesus claimed to be the King of the Jews

At the time of Jesus, Israel was a tiny colony controlled by the massive Roman Empire. The Jews believed that someday a Messiah figure would be sent by God to help them drive the Roman government from their country. They believed their Messiah was to be a King—the "King of the Jews," also referred to as the "Son of David." Of course, the Roman government didn't like the idea of a Jewish Messiah because the Messiah's job (so the Jews believed) was to oust the Roman government from the country and establish a Jewish government *in its place.* Ultimately then, the Roman government crucified Jesus because of the accusation put forward by the Jewish religious authorities—that He was claiming to be the King of the Jews (Jesus agreed to this title even though He had no intentions of waging political warfare or establishing a worldly form of government). From the Roman government's perspective, accepting the title "King of the Jews" was tantamount to committing treason. And of course, treason was punishable by crucifixion.

2. Jesus claimed to be God

Throughout the course of His three-year ministry, Jesus did and said many things that gave the impression He was claiming to be the one God of Israel. For example, He used God's name for Himself (He referred to Himself as "I Am"), He forgave sins that were committed against God, He referred to

Himself as "Lord of the Sabbath," He said, "I and the Father are one" and "whoever has seen Me has seen the Father" and so on. The Jewish religious leaders (the scribes, the Pharisees and the Sadducees) were convinced that by saying and doing these things Jesus was committing the sin of blasphemy. The bible prescribes the death penalty (stoning) for such a sin.

The Jewish religious leaders avoided stoning Jesus because they were controlled by the Roman government and as such had to defer to Roman law which stipulated death by crucifixion for crimes against the state. Blasphemy however, simply wasn't a crime against the Roman state. In fact it had nothing to do with Roman law! The Jews therefore approached the Roman governor of Judea, Pontius Pilate, and demanded that Jesus be crucified for claiming to be King of the Jews (treason). When Pontius Pilate asked "are you the King of the Jews?" Jesus responded: "You say so" (Matt 27:11). He also responded:

> My kingdom does not belong to this world. If my kingdom did belong to this world, my attendants [would] be fighting to keep me from being handed over to the Jews. But as it is, my kingdom is not here (John 18:36).

Jesus' answer likely convinced Pilate that He was a harmless dreamer. Pilate returned to the Jews with his verdict—not guilty! Nevertheless, the Jews persisted and demanded that Jesus be crucified. Pilate ultimately gave into the crowd because he was afraid they might (a) begin a riot, which could easily erupt into a full-scale war, and (b) report him to the Roman Emperor for letting a potentially treasonous person off the hook. That would certainly end his career as governor.

The Crucifixion: The Ultimate Act Of Obedience

So, Jesus was crucified for "committing" treason and blasphemy. But in what way was His Crucifixion an act of obedience?

When questioned by the Jewish religious leaders about His identity, Jesus could have taken the easy way out; He could have *lied* and said, "you've got the wrong guy! I'm not God." Similarly, He could have lied to the Romans and said, "nope, I'm definitely not the King of the Jews." If He simply *lied* about His identity He could have saved His life and spared Himself from a gruesome death.

If Jesus lied however, that lie would be an act of disobedience against the Eight Commandment: "thou shalt not bear false witness against your neighbor." The fact is, He *was* the King of the Jews and He *was* God. He had to remain true to Himself, for in denying Himself He would cease to be Himself, and as the bible says, God "cannot lie" (Hebrews 6:18) and "cannot deny Himself" (2 Timothy 2:13). Jesus' Crucifixion then, was an act of intense obedience to the truth of His own identity. Thus, the Crucifixion— the possibility of having to die for the truth— provided Jesus with a situation where it would be extremely difficult for Him to be obedient and as such, it enabled Him to demonstrate/offer intense obedience to God the Father.

Three Reasons For Jesus' Crucifixion In Sum

1. God the Father required Jesus to be Crucified because it was the only circumstance available in the ancient world that provided Jesus with the opportunity to fully demonstrate the <u>extent</u> of His obedience. This level of obedience was needed to rebalance the scales of justice.
2. The Jewish religious leaders required Jesus' death because they believed He was guilty of blasphemy.
3. The Roman government required Jesus' Crucifixion because of the charge of treason being levied against Him.

Death Is The Last Phase Of Life

As we know, God's plan of salvation was to LIVE a life of perfect human obedience in order to counterbalance the sins of the world. Nevertheless, as evidenced by the biblical quotes at the head of this chapter, we can see that Christianity attributes a human's salvation to Jesus' death. So which is it? Are humans saved by Jesus' *life* of obedience, or by His obedient *death*?

In reality, life and death are part of the same continuum; they are not two completely separate events. Death is the last phase of life; it is something each and every soul must experience or *live through.* Death then, belongs to the category of life. Thus, to say that we are saved by Jesus' death, is not to contradict the statement that we are saved by His life.

The Separation Of The Soul From The Body

Technically speaking, death is the separation of the soul from the body. If we are saved merely by the separation of Jesus' soul from His body, then why the need for the Crucifixion? Why not a natural death? You see, ultimately it is not merely Jesus' death, in and of itself, that saves us. As we will discover below, it is Jesus' obedience that saves us!

Saved By Jesus' Death

The New Testament is adamant that we are saved by the death of Jesus. This has to be understood. It does not mean that that Jesus' death in and of itself (the separation of His human soul from His human body) is what saves mankind. Rather, in saying that we are saved by Jesus' death the bible means that we are saved by Jesus' intense obedience which He displayed *while He was dying on the Cross.* This is why the prophet Isaiah, speaking seven hundred years before the Crucifixion said that the Messiah would save us "By making his LIFE as a reparation offering" (Is 53:10, emphasis added).

Saved By Jesus' Blood

The New Testament also teaches that we are saved by Jesus' blood! Again, this does not mean that Jesus' blood, in and of itself, is what saves us. No!

This statement means that we are saved by Jesus' obedience which He displayed *while He shed His blood on the Cross*.

Saved By Jesus' Suffering

The New Testament also teaches that we are saved by Jesus' suffering. Of course, this does not mean that Jesus' suffering, in and of itself, is what saves humans. Rather, this means that we are saved by Jesus' obedience, which He displayed *while suffering on the Cross*.

Saved By Jesus' Obedience

So, whether we say we are saved by Jesus' "life" or "death" or by His "suffering" or by His "blood" makes no difference. All these statements are true. It must be understood however that ultimately it is Jesus' obedience that saves—His obedience while living, His obedience while dying (the last phase of life), His obedience while suffering, His obedience while shedding His blood. As the Catholic Catechism affirms, it is "the obedience of Jesus, which achieves our salvation" (CCC 1850). With that said, the scriptures, and Christian tradition stress Jesus' death as the ultimate basis for our salvation because it was during His death that He demonstrated the extent of His human obedience.

Jesus' One Life?

One very important question that needs to be addressed is, "how could Jesus' *one* life of perfect human obedience make up for millions, even billions of disobedient lives"? The answer has to do with who Jesus is. Even though Jesus had a human nature, He was still God. This caused His *human* life to become infinitely valuable. And since His one human life carried infinite weight/value/significance, it was able to outweigh all of the millions, even billions of sinful lives, thus rebalancing the scales of Justice.

PRAYER

Jesus, it must have been so difficult for you to keep your divinity a secret! Of course, you had to! You knew how people would react if you told them the whole truth about your identity. They would think you were crazy, or a blasphemer. Of course this is what ended up happening...and they put you to death. Still, all those years and the only people who knew that you were God were your dear Mother Mary and foster father Joseph. It must have been comforting to have them to talk to, at least! Thank you Jesus for living through your death with such intense obedience. You could have denied your divinity and your kingship, but you didn't. You remained completely obedient to the truth, right to the very end. And because of your intense obedience, now I have the chance to be saved. Please fill my heart and mind with the awareness of all you have done...and may I ponder your awesome plan of salvation all the days of my life. Amen!

Questions:

1. Why was Jesus required to perform an act of intense obedience?
2. What is it that can make obedience more intense and hence more valuable to God?
3. Why could Jesus not have saved us by stubbing His toe, or by pricking His finger, or even by dying a natural death?
4. Why was it necessary for Jesus to be crucified?
5. Which commandment would Jesus have broken if He lied about His identity in order to escape Crucifixion?
6. What are the three reasons for Jesus' Crucifixion?
7. Explain how death can actually belong to the category of life?
8. What is death?
9. Catholics say that we are saved by Jesus' blood, suffering, life and death. How can all of these disparate statements be reconciled?

CHAPTER 19
BAPTISM: ELEVATING HUMAN NATURE

"God is in no way, directly or indirectly, the cause of moral evil. He permits it, however, because he respects the freedom of his creatures and, mysteriously, knows how to derive good from it..." (CCC 311).

"Or are you unaware that we who were baptized into Christ Jesus were baptized into his death? We were indeed buried with him through baptism into death, so that, just as Christ was raised from the dead by the glory of the Father, we too might live in newness of life. For if we have grown into union with him through a death like his, we shall also be united with him in the resurrection" (Romans 6:3-5).

"For if by the transgression of the one, death reigned through the one, much more those who receive the abundance of grace and of the gift of righteousness will reign in life through the One, Jesus Christ" (Romans 5:17).

"All of us, gazing with unveiled face on the glory of the Lord, are being transformed into the same image from glory to glory, as from the Lord who is the Spirit" (2 Corinthians 3:18).

"So whoever is in Christ is a new creation: the old things have passed away; behold, new things have come" (2 Corinthians 5:17).

"You were buried with him in baptism, in which you were also raised with him through faith in the power of God, who raised him from the dead. And even when you were dead [in] transgressions and the uncircumcision of your flesh, he brought you to life along with him, having forgiven us all our transgressions..." (Colossians 2:12-13).

> "But God, who is rich in mercy, because of the great love he had for us, even when we were dead in our transgressions, brought us to life with Christ (by grace you have been saved), raised us up with him, and seated us with him in the heavens in Christ Jesus.." (Ephesians 2:4-6).
>
> "His divine power has bestowed on us everything that makes for life and devotion...so that through them you may come **to share in the divine nature**, after escaping from the corruption that is in the world because of evil desire" (1 Peter 1:3-4).
>
> "Like obedient children, do not act in compliance with the desires of your former ignorance but, as he who called you is holy, be holy yourselves in every aspect of your conduct, for it is written, "Be holy because I [am] holy" (1 Pet 1:14-16).
>
> "Mortal sin is a radical possibility of human freedom, as is love itself. It results in the loss of charity and the privation of sanctifying grace, that is, of the state of grace. If it is not redeemed by repentance and God's forgiveness, it causes exclusion from Christ's kingdom and the eternal death of hell, for our freedom has the power to make choices for ever, with no turning back. However, although we can judge that an act is in itself a grave offense, we must entrust judgment of persons to the justice and mercy of God" (CCC 1861).

Healing Human Nature After Settling The Debt

The life and death of Jesus (His death being the last phase of His life and His most intense expression of human obedience) rebalanced the universal scales of justice by giving to God the Father the loving obedience that was due Him since the Original Sin. While Jesus' life and death solved the problem of an out of balance scales of justice, it didn't necessarily, or automatically heal humanity's fallen nature or raise mankind to participate in the divine nature. Despite Jesus' death on the Cross then, human nature remained in its fallen state and mankind remained separated from friendship and intimacy with God. In this chapter, we will look at how God planned to fix the human nature of individuals by raising them to participate in His own blessed life.

'O Happy Fault'

It may be that God's original plan was to make Adam and Eve share in His own blessed life once they passed the "test" posed by the Tree of the Knowledge of Good and Evil. How that was to be achieved we do not know, but in any event, they failed the test. Yet, the Church refers to the sin of our first parents as a "happy fault." This is because it resulted in God's decision to fix or heal human nature not by returning it to its state of Original Holiness and Justice, but by completely elevating it to the divine status! When Adam and Eve sinned, you could almost imagine God saying the following:

> "Don't think you can get away with this Satan. You can't do that to my humans. I'll show you. You think you can distort my image and likeness in mankind, but I'll do something you never even thought possible. I'll make them even higher than they were originally. I'm going to graft humans onto/into my own being so that they become sharers in my own divine nature."

The Complete System Upgrade

When a computer system becomes corrupted with a virus for example, we can fix it with a "patch." These patches are designed not only to fix the issue, but to upgrade the entire computer system. Fallen human nature (that is, the "in Adam" nature) is similar to a computer system infected by a virus known as Original Sin. To fix human nature, God designed His own kind of "patch"—baptism. Far from restoring man to his pre-fallen condition of Original Holiness and Justice, baptism would begin a "system upgrade" in humans, a transmogrification into the divine status.

Upgrade Not Automatically Applied To Everyone

Even though Jesus' life of perfect loving human obedience rebalanced the universal scales of Justice by giving God the Father His due, His obedience is not automatically credited to any individual's account, so to speak. Oftentimes—for a great variety of reasons—this is because people don't believe they need Jesus' life of obedience to make up for their disobedience. Their rejection of Jesus' saving work is not necessarily based on a hatred or dislike for Jesus Himself. Quite often, non-Christians simply don't accept the premise that humans are hopelessly in debt to God and in need of a savior in the first place.

How To Make Jesus' Obedience Count For You

Even if—hypothetically speaking—every human being rejected the Crucifixion of Jesus...if the Crucifixion was only ever met with coldhearted dismissal, it would still be effective as an act of reparation for the sins of the world. Put another way, regardless of its influence on humans, the Crucifixion served to satisfy the justice of God and rebalance the scales of justice.

Nevertheless, for Jesus' obedience to "count" against an *individual's* sins, the following must take place:

a) You must have a *sincere faith* that Jesus' obedience compensates for your sins
b) You must have *true sorrow* for your disobedience towards God
c) You must desire to unite yourself to Jesus (to be "in Christ")
d) You must demonstrate *true repentance* (turning away from sin) and your desire to be "in Christ" by being baptized and doing your best to avoid sin until your physical death. By avoiding sin, you ensure that you remain "in Christ."

Baptism

In baptism an individual's spirit becomes united to Christ (becomes "in Christ") thereby experiencing the "system upgrade." Anyone who is baptized therefore, has truly started down the path of coming to share in the divine nature. Without baptism:

(a) Jesus' life of obedience cannot be used to count against your disobedience
(b) The "system upgrade" (normally initiated in baptism) does not *begin* in you

(c) You remain "in Adam" (in a fully fallen state)

What Happens In Baptism

The act of going under and rising out of the waters of baptism symbolizes:

(a) our dying with Jesus
(b) being buried with Jesus
(c) rising with Jesus

But this "dying with," being "buried with" and "rising with" Jesus does not mean that we somehow die *alongside* Jesus, are buried *alongside* Him or rise *alongside* Him. No! In baptism we become united with Jesus such that *we* experience *His* death, *His* burial and *His* resurrection as our very own. Now if, by faith, we have truly united ourselves to Jesus (sacramentally) in His obedient death, then His intensely obedient death becomes our own and counts as much for us as it did for Him. Jesus' obedience however, can only be credited to an individual's account if that individual becomes united to Him. Through baptism then, our disobedient (fallen) spirit dies and comes alive with the holiness and justice of Christ.

Similarly, the act of rising out of the water symbolizes our rising with Christ. But again, when we say that we rise "with" Christ we do not mean to suggest that we rise "alongside" Him. Rather, by virtue of being united with Jesus through faith, we experience His resurrection as our own. This is precisely why the New Testament teaches that "whoever is in Christ" has been "raised up" and is "seated" with Jesus "in the heavens" (Eph 2:6).

Before Original Sin	After Original Sin "In Adam"	After Baptism: "In Christ"
Human Nature 1.0 Original Holiness, Justice and Innocence	Fallen Nature 0.5 Inclination to sin Eventual physical death	Divinized Nature 2.0 Process of complete system upgrade underway

Complete System Upgrade: A Two-Step Process

Anyone who knows about fixing computers will confirm that after a patch has been installed the ENTIRE computer must be shut down in order for the update to take effect. Upon restarting, the computer will begin to operate as an upgraded version of its former self. Baptism works along the very same lines: only that which is shut down (i.e., dies) can experience the system upgrade...

The New Testament teaches that in baptism, a person's "old self" (sprit) dies and comes alive again. This is because baptism causes a person's spirit only to be united to Jesus in His death, burial and resurrection. But since baptism doesn't unite a person's body to Jesus in His death, burial and resurrection, the body cannot experience any upgrade. Put another way, since the body doesn't die in baptism, it cannot undergo a regeneration or upgrade. The upgrade happens to a person's spirit only because only the spirit dies in baptism. The body will *eventually* experience the upgrade—on the last day—but first, it has to die.

Through baptism then, a person's spirit experiences death, burial, resurrection, re-generation and divinization while his/her body remains in its fallen, un-regenerated and un-resurrected state. To put it simply, after baptism, a person's spirit is "in Christ" but his body is still rooted "in Adam." A baptized person therefore, is only HALF DIVINIZED—united to Christ in spirit, but still "fallen" in body. The spirit has experienced the upgrade, but the body is still stuck in the old mode of fallen-ness. While baptism brings about the divinization of the spirit, raising it to 2.0, the body stays in its un-resurrected, un-regenerated state, at the level of 0.5.

Experiencing a COMPLETE system upgrade then, is really a two-step process, the first step being baptism, and the second step being the resurrection of the dead body on the last day. While we await the COMPLETE system upgrade, it is as if our human nature is "buffering."

Feeling Un-Resurrected
Since baptism does not completely get rid of Original Sin (it lingers in the un-resurrected body) life after baptism can seem pretty much the same as life before baptism. We still sin, we still feel guilty, we still struggle etc. Being present and active in the body, Original Sin persists in dragging the spirit downward to disobedience. The baptized Christian thus lives in constant inner conflict and tension, dragged between two worlds. It is as if one foot is in heaven (the spirit) while the other is on earth (the

body). The newly divinized and resurrected spirit desires spiritual things while the un-resurrected body (what the bible calls "the flesh") continues to desire the things of the world. The newly divinized spirit desires to be obedient to God (Matt 26:41) while the body wants to perform the same old acts of disobedience it always has. In the book of Romans, St. Paul teaches that we need not be overcome by this daily struggle, but can experience success over our desires to sin:

> We know that our old self was crucified with him, so that our sinful body might be done away with, that we might no longer be in slavery to sin (Rom 6:6).

How To Live In The Spirit

The bible teaches that we can experience the joy of heaven within us if we learn to deny the sinful desires of the body. Rather than being directed by what the bible calls the "desires of the flesh" we should learn to follow the desires of the Holy Spirit who lives within us. As St. Paul states in his letter to the Galatians, "I say, then: live by the Spirit and you will certainly not gratify the desire of the flesh" (Ch. 5:16). This is a daily battle we must all fight. But the more we practice living by the Spirit, the easier it will become.

PRAYER

Oh Lord Jesus, I am amazed at the wonder of Baptism! In this sacrament, you took me a sinner and united me to you in your death, burial and resurrection! I was submerged into you and am now united with you in spirit. The scriptures say that I am currently seated with you in heaven, blessed with every spiritual blessing in the heavenly realms. It all seems so mysterious to me. I can hardly get over the fact that in my spirit, I am united to you and that because of our unity, my spirit is sharing in your divinity. I am certainly on the path to fulfilling my destiny and it is wonderful to me! For now, I have to deal with my tendencies to sin, which obviously don't come from being united to you, but come from the fallen body (the flesh) that I carry with me. Help me Lord Jesus to live a life worthy of the calling I have received and to do everything in my power to follow the leadings and promptings of your most Holy Spirit. Amen!

Questions:

1. Why does Jesus' death not automatically save the whole world?
2. What do people need to do to benefit from Jesus' saving work?
3. What do we need to do, as baptized individuals, to stay "in Christ"?
4. What is it that dies, specifically, in Baptism?
5. Why does the body not experience a "system upgrade" through Baptism?
6. Explain why every baptized Christian experiences inner conflict.
7. Baptism causes the system upgrade to *begin*. Explain what needs to happen before the entire upgrade takes place.

CHAPTER 20
THE REDEMPTION

"This sacrifice of Christ is unique; it completes and surpasses all other sacrifices. First, it is a gift from God the Father himself, for the Father handed his Son over to sinners in order to reconcile us with himself. At the same time it is the offering of the Son of God made man, who in freedom and love offered his life to his Father through the Holy Spirit in reparation for our disobedience" (CCC 614).

Jesus substitutes His obedience for our disobedience
"For as by one man's disobedience many were made sinners, so by one man's obedience many will be made righteous." By his obedience unto death, Jesus accomplished the substitution of the suffering Servant, who "makes himself an offering for sin", when "he bore the sin of many", and who "shall make many to be accounted righteous", for "he shall bear their iniquities". Jesus atoned for our faults and made satisfaction for our sins to the Father" (CCC 615).

"We cannot be united with God unless we freely choose to love him. But we cannot love God if we sin gravely against him, against our neighbor or against ourselves... To die in mortal sin without repenting and accepting God's merciful love means remaining separated from him forever by our own free choice. This state of definitive self-exclusion from communion with God and the blessed is called "hell" (CCC 1033).

"God predestines no one to go to hell; for this, a willful turning away from God (a mortal sin) is necessary, and persistence in it until the end. In the Eucharistic liturgy and in the daily prayers of her faithful, the Church implores the mercy of God, who does not want any to perish, but all to come to repentance" (CCC 1037).

A Popular Non-Catholic View Of Redemption

A number of non-Catholic Christian denominations (Evangelicals, Baptists and Pentecostals for example) hold an almost completely different version of redemption than that of the Catholic Church. Learning what these churches believe should lead to a clearer understanding of Catholic teaching.

The prevailing non-Catholic Christian view states that Adam and Eve's sin caused humanity to become the legal property of the devil. That is, by getting Adam and Eve to sin, the devil won legal rights to their souls and the souls of every human who would ever be born. It is as if when they sinned, the devil became the jail keeper (hell being the jail) and all humans became his rightful prisoners who he won fair and square.

In addition, this non-Catholic Christian view holds that God was legally required to give some kind of ransom TO THE DEVIL in order to redeem (buy back) mankind from his evil clutches. That ransom, in basic terms (for now) was Jesus. Thus, God handed Jesus over to the devil as legal payment to buy humanity back. And so, humans were set free from hell because Jesus went there in our place.

Besides simply taking the place of humans in hell (to become the devil's legal property) the prevailing non-Catholic Christian view of redemption teaches that Jesus was also *punished* in hell by God the Father. So, not only did Jesus occupy hell so we wouldn't have to, but He also took on all the punishments that humans would have received there. This theory—that Jesus was punished in our place—is known as substitutionary atonement.

Of course, hell is a "place" of *eternal* punishment. All souls who go there are there for good. In order for Jesus to truly take on the punishments of hell, He would have had to stay there forever. But since He was raised from the dead on the "third day" those who hold to this non-Catholic view of redemption conclude that Jesus must have experienced the equivalent of an eternity in hell in the day and a half He spent there. In addition, the punishments that were inflicted on Jesus in hell, according to the abovementioned theory, were inflicted by none other than God the Father. Hell, after all, is the place where God *punishes* sinners. Thus, while in hell, Jesus experienced an eternity's worth of God the Father's wrath.

This non-Catholic view of redemption also holds that Jesus' experience of eternal punishment began not after His death, but on the Cross. This means that as Jesus was being Crucified He was living through a hell of sorts, taking on mankind's punishment and enduring the anger of God the Father.

Infusion Of Sinfulness And Guilt

But how could God the Father get angry with Jesus, the innocent Lamb of God? How could He unleash His wrath on His only begotten Son? The answer is that

Jesus also took into His Being the sinfulness and guilt of humanity. That is, He literally *became guilty* of mankind's sins. It is as if His pure, innocent soul became filled with all guilt and every wickedness. According to this non-Catholic view, Jesus wasn't the innocent guy taking the rap for our sins; He *became the sinner*, infused with true sinfulness and guilt. In fact, because He took into Himself all the sins of every sinner who ever lived and who would ever live, He became the most sinful person to ever exist. This is why, according to this non-Catholic view, God the Father became angry with His only begotten Son! As Martin Luther, one of the first Protestant reformers once wrote:

> Whatever sins I, you, and all of us have committed or may commit in the future, they are as much Christ's own as if he himself had committed them. In short, our sin must be Christ's own sin, or we shall perish eternally (Luther's Works).

And in another place, he wrote the following:

> And all the prophets saw this, that Christ was to become the greatest thief, murderer, adulterer, robber, desecrator, blasphemer, etc., there has ever been anywhere in the world. ... In short, he has and bears all the sins of all men in his body (Luther's Works).

Ultimately however—according to this non-Catholic view—since Jesus hadn't *personally* committed any sin, hell could not hold Him captive, and He rose from the dead on the third day!

The Catholic View Of Redemption

The following points sum up the Catholic understanding of redemption and will serve to contrast with the standard non-Catholic Christian view outlined above:

a) Jesus saved us by taking on a human nature and living a life of perfect loving human obedience, the high point of which was the Crucifixion, where He demonstrated extreme obedience to God the Father which obedience offset the disobedience of humanity and counterbalanced the universal scales of justice.

b) Jesus saves us by uniting us to His death, burial and resurrection through the waters of baptism in order to initiate the process of divinization and achieve the goal for which we were created—to "share in His blessed life."

c) Jesus saved humanity by paying a ransom TO GOD THE FATHER and not to the devil! That ransom was His own life of perfect loving human obedience, the culmination of which was His Crucifixion.

d) When Jesus was dying on the Cross He remained completely holy and innocent. As the innocent Lamb of God He offered His perfect loving obedience to God the Father while being sacrificed for His obedience to the truth of His own identity.

e) Jesus' extreme obedience was the ransom/payment that would buy humans back NOT FROM THE DEVIL, but from our position of debt to God the Father.

f) When God the Father saw the depths of His Son's obedience He was moved to pity (not wrath) and was willing not only to forgive humans for their sins but to infuse—through baptism—His own Being and holiness into the souls of those who would believe in Jesus and be baptized.

The Catholic Church teaches that those who unite to Jesus through baptism literally have Jesus' own being and holiness infused into their souls. And anyone who has Jesus' holiness in his/her soul is called a "saint," a term which means "made holy."

PRAYER

Dear Jesus, when I think of what you did for humanity I am filled with wonder and awe. You settled our debt with God the Father by providing for Him an act of extreme obedience, which act cost you your human life. Your human life was the ransom which you paid to God the Father to redeem us from our debt of obedience. You were the most innocent Lamb of God, pouring out your love on behalf of all humans, even though you knew that not everyone would accept your sacrifice as a means of salvation. May I always be inspired by your sacrifice to live a better life and strive towards a greater depth of love. Amen!

WHY JESUS HAD TO BE CRUCIFIED

CHAPTER 21
DESCENDED INTO HELL

"Scripture calls the abode of the dead, to which the dead Christ went down, "hell" - Sheol in Hebrew or Hades in Greek - because those who are there are deprived of the vision of God. Such is the case for all the dead, whether evil or righteous, while they await the Redeemer: which does not mean that their lot is identical, as Jesus shows through the parable of the poor man Lazarus who was received into "Abraham's bosom": "It is precisely these holy souls, who awaited their Savior in Abraham's bosom, whom Christ the Lord delivered when he descended into hell." Jesus did not descend into hell to deliver the damned, nor to destroy the hell of damnation, but to free the just who had gone before him" (CCC 633).

The Apostles' Creed

The Apostles' Creed states that Jesus "descended into hell." Is this proof that Jesus actually *did* go to hell? Simply put, the answer is "no." The early Christians never used the word "hell" to refer to a place of eternal punishment, or eternal separation from God. Rather, when the Apostles' Creed was written, the word "hell" was frequently used to refer to the place where all the good souls from the Old Testament went. The meaning of "hell" has obviously changed dramatically over the years!

Two Sections Of Sheol – Paradise And Gehenna

In the Old Testament, or any time before Jesus' Crucifixion, anyone who died went to a place called "Sheol," also known as the "Abode of the Dead."

Sheol was believed to have two sections, one for the good souls ("The Bosom of Abraham") and one for the wicked souls ("Gehenna"). The early Christian Church however, simply referred to the Bosom of Abraham as "hell!" For the early Christians then, "hell" was actually a *good* place. It wasn't until much later that Christians began to use the word "hell" to refer to Gehenna, the wicked section of Sheol, the place of eternal punishment.

Jesus explained that there was a "chasm" (gap) between the two sections of Sheol (Luke 16:26). The purpose of the chasm was to prevent souls in Gehenna from crossing into the Bosom of Abraham. The souls in Gehenna were there for good. They would never be able to graduate out of it. The souls who went to the Bosom of Abraham, on the other hand, were the good guys. Eventually, they would enter into heaven! But before that could happen, their Messiah would have to come and free them.

Heaven In The Old Testament
The Old Testament seems to indicate that some people (very few) were able to completely bypass Sheol altogether and go straight to heaven. One such person was Enoch (Gen 5:24) and possibly Moses and Elijah. However, most people from the Old Testament went to Sheol—either the Gehenna section, or Bosom of Abraham section.

Today You Will Be With Me In Paradise

The intertestamental book of Esdras reveals that the Jews also referred to the Bosom of Abraham as "paradise" (2 Esdras 7:36). This means that before Christians began to refer to the good section of Sheol as "hell," the Jews had been calling it both the "Bosom of Abraham" and "Paradise." This helps us to understand what Jesus meant when He said to the man being crucified next to Him: "...today you will be with me in paradise." Many make the mistake of thinking Jesus meant they would see each other in heaven as soon as they died. In modern English, Jesus basically said, "I'll see you in the Bosom of Abraham pretty soon."

What Did Jesus Do When He Was "Dead"?

The New Testament informs us that when Jesus died, He went to the Bosom of Abraham—the Old Testament waiting place for righteous souls (referred to by Jesus as "paradise")—to rescue the good souls who were there! While there, Jesus directed these good souls to heaven! As we read in 1 Peter 3:18:

> [When Jesus was] Put to death in the flesh, he was brought to life in the spirit. In the Spirit, he also went to preach to the spirits in prison..

This "prison" Peter refers to is the Bosom of Abraham/paradise.

PRAYER

Lord Jesus, I am amazed to learn that Adam and Eve and all the righteous souls who lived before your Crucifixion were taken care of by you in the Bosom of Abraham. You took care even of those righteous souls who may have lived during Noah's flood! I am so happy to learn that you visited them after your soul separated from your human body and set them free to enter into heaven. Even after your physical death, you never stopped working for the salvation of the human race. Thank you Jesus for your enduring love for all of us. I ask you that every person on this planet would open themselves to your love so that they might have true faith in your Crucifixion and enter into the waters of baptism. Amen!

Questions:

1. List the various names for the place where Jesus went when He died on the Cross.
2. What did Jesus mean when He said to the man crucified beside Him, "today you will be with me in paradise"?
3. What do you think of the fact that the word "hell" has undergone such a radical change in meaning?
4. What are the two sections of Sheol and what was the purpose of each?
5. Was it possible for souls to migrate from one section of Sheol to the other? Explain your answer.

CHAPTER 22
THE MASS: KEEPING THE SCALES OF JUSTICE IN BALANCE

"For there is no distinction; all have sinned and are deprived of the glory of God. They are justified freely by his grace through the redemption in Christ Jesus, whom God set forth as an expiation, through faith, by his blood, to prove his righteousness because of **THE FORGIVENESS OF SINS PREVIOUSLY COMMITTED**, through the forbearance of God—to prove his righteousness in the present time, that he might be righteous and justify the one who has faith in Jesus" (Romans 3:22-26).

"The memorial of the Lord's Passion and Resurrection: The Holy Sacrifice, because it **makes present the one sacrifice of Christ** the Savior and includes the Church's offering. The terms holy sacrifice of the Mass, "sacrifice of praise," spiritual sacrifice, pure and holy sacrifice are also used, since it completes and surpasses all the sacrifices of the Old Covenant" (CCC 1330).

"At the heart of the Eucharistic celebration are the bread and wine that, by the words of Christ and the invocation of the Holy Spirit, become Christ's Body and Blood" (CCC 1333).

"We carry out this command of the Lord by celebrating the memorial of his sacrifice. In so doing, we offer to the Father what he has himself given us: the gifts of his creation, bread and wine which, by the power of the Holy Spirit and by the words of Christ, have become the body and blood of Christ. Christ is thus really and mysteriously made present" (CCC 1357).

"The Eucharist is the memorial of Christ's Passover, the making present and the sacramental offering of his unique sacrifice, in *the liturgy of the Church which is his Body" (CCC 1362).*

"In the New Testament, the memorial takes on new meaning. When the Church celebrates the Eucharist, she commemorates Christ's Passover, and it is made present the sacrifice Christ offered once for all on the cross remains ever present. "As often as the sacrifice of the Cross by which 'Christ our Pasch has been sacrificed' is celebrated on the altar, the work of our redemption is carried out" (CCC 1364).

"Because it is the memorial of Christ's Passover, the Eucharist is also a sacrifice. The sacrificial character of the Eucharist is manifested in the very words of institution: "This is my body which is given for you" and "This cup which is poured out for you is the New Covenant in my blood." In the Eucharist Christ gives us the very body which he gave up for us on the cross, the very blood which he "poured out for many for the forgiveness of sins" (CCC 1365).

"The sacrifice of Christ and the sacrifice of the Eucharist are one single sacrifice: "The victim is one and the same: the same now offers through the ministry of priests, who then offered himself on the cross; only the manner of offering is different." "And since in this divine sacrifice which is celebrated in the Mass, the same Christ who offered himself once in a bloody manner on the altar of the cross is contained and is offered in an unbloody manner... this sacrifice is truly propitiatory" (CCC 1367).

"The Eucharist is also the sacrifice of the Church. The Church which is the Body of Christ participates in the offering of her Head. With him, she herself is offered whole and entire. She unites herself to his intercession with the Father for all men. In the Eucharist the sacrifice of Christ becomes also the sacrifice of the members of his Body. The lives of the faithful, their praise, sufferings, prayer, and work, are united with those of Christ and with his total offering, and so acquire a new value. Christ's sacrifice present on the altar makes it possible for all

generations of Christians to be united with his offering" (CCC 1368).

"The mode of Christ's presence under the Eucharistic species is unique. It raises the Eucharist above all the sacraments as "the perfection of the spiritual life and the end to which all the sacraments tend." In the most blessed sacrament of the Eucharist "the body and blood, together with the soul and divinity, of our Lord Jesus Christ and, therefore, the whole Christ is truly, really, and substantially contained." "This presence is called 'real' – by which is not intended to exclude the other types of presence as if they could not be 'real' too, but because it is presence in the fullest sense: that is to say, it is a substantial presence by which Christ, God and man, makes himself wholly and entirely present" (CCC 1374).

"Pray, my sisters and brothers, that your sacrifice and mine may be acceptable to God the Almighty Father." ""May the Lord accept the sacrifice at your hands for the praise and glory of His name, for our good and the good of all His holy Church" (The Liturgy of the Eucharist).

"...but he, because he remains forever, has a priesthood that does not pass away" (Hebrews 7:24).

"For Christ did not enter into a sanctuary made by hands, a copy of the true one, but heaven itself, that he might now appear before God on our behalf. Not that he might offer himself repeatedly, as the high priest enters each year into the sanctuary with blood that is not his own; if that were so, he would have had to suffer repeatedly from the foundation of the world. But now once for all he has appeared at the end of the ages to take away sin by his sacrifice" (Hebrews 9:24-26).

Sin After The Crucifixion

Jesus' life of perfect loving human obedience (especially His death) fully compensated God the Father for all the disobedience committed since the beginning of the world and completely balanced the scales of Justice, making it possible for God to *justly* forgive sins and unite people to Him. After the Crucifixion however, people continued to sin. By these sins, individual humans once again failed to give God the perfect loving obedience He deserves and once again placed themselves into a position of debt towards God—a debt that would be impossible to pay because of the fallen human condition.

Jesus' Crucifixion, while infinite in its *power* to counterbalance all sins—past present and future—was only applied towards offsetting/counterbalancing those sins that were committed *before* the Crucifixion. As St. Paul states:

> ...the redemption in Christ Jesus, whom God set forth as an expiation, through faith, by his blood, to prove his righteousness because of the forgiveness of **SINS PREVIOUSLY COMMITTED**... (Rom 3:25, emphasis added)

Dealing With Post-Crucifixion Sins

Again, while Jesus' Crucifixion two thousand years ago certainly had the *power* to make up for all sins, (past, present and future) its saving effects, at the time of the Crucifixion, were applied only to "sins previously committed" (Rom 3:25). In order for the

WHY JESUS HAD TO BE CRUCIFIED

saving effects of Jesus' Crucifixion to apply to sins committed after the Cross, His Crucifixion would have to be re-presented to God the Father. This is accomplished at the Catholic Mass which, as the Catholic Catechism puts it, is...

> ...the memorial of Christ's Passover, **the making present** and the **sacramental offering** of his unique sacrifice in the liturgy of the Church... (CCC 1362, emphasis added).

Re-Presented, NOT Represent

It is important to use the correct terminology when describing what happens at Mass. The word "re-present" is used to describe the re-offering of the Sacrifice of Jesus rather than the word "represent" (CCC 1366). This is because the Mass is not some kind of symbolic representation of Jesus' death. It truly is the SAME Sacrifice of two thousand years ago being presented to God the Father in real-time. To put it in modern terms, offering the Catholic Mass is like hitting the "refresh" button on Jesus' Sacrifice.

The Mass: The Work Of Redemption

Because the Sacrifice of the Mass is the same Sacrifice that was offered two thousand years ago, albeit in an un-bloody manner and through the agency of the Catholic priesthood, it counterbalances human disobedience in the same way it did back in the time of Jesus! It should come as no surprise then that the Church teaches that Mass is offered so that "its saving grace [may] be applied to the remission of those sins which we daily commit..." (DS 938). In addition, the Catholic Catechism teaches that:

> As often as the sacrifice of the Cross by which 'Christ our Pasch has been sacrificed' is celebrated on the altar, the **work of our redemption is carried out** (CCC 1364, emphasis added).

The Historical And The Sacramental

When Jesus was Crucified two thousand years ago, His obedience was used to counterbalance all the disobedient acts that were committed up to that point in time—including Adam and Eve's act of Original Sin (which caused the fallen human condition known as "Original Sin"). When the first Mass after the Crucifixion was offered, it compensated God for the sins that were committed *since Jesus' historical Sacrifice*. Today, whenever a Mass is offered, the effect is the same—it compensates God for any and all sins committed *since the last Mass*.

Forgiveness And The Mass

The "compensation" rendered to God by the historical Sacrifice of Jesus, enabled Him to JUSTLY extend forgiveness for all sins committed up till that point. And inasmuch as the Mass is Jesus' Sacrifice—in real time—we can conclude that the Mass forms the basis for God's just forgiveness of sins (in the sacrament of Confession). That is, each Mass makes God's daily forgiveness of sins possible and just. The liturgy truly is the "font from which all her [the Church] power flows" (*Sacrosanctum Concilium*, 10).

When Does The Sacrifice Take Place?

To be exact, the Sacrifice of Jesus is made present when the priest (acting in the Person of Christ) consecrates the bread and wine. He does this by speaking the words, "this is my Body" and "this is the Chalice of my Blood." The Catholic Encyclopedia confirms this, speaking of the "the act of sacrifice (*actio sacrifica*), veiled in the double consecration..." After performing two separate consecrations, the priest takes Jesus' Body in one hand and Jesus' Blood in the other. By holding them in separate hands the priest dramatizes Jesus' death which is naturally implied by the separation of a person's body and blood. Finally, the priest elevates Jesus' Body and Blood above the altar to symbolize that he, playing the part of Jesus, is offering Christ's death to God the Father, who is in heaven.

The Host

The primary function of any altar is to provide a surface upon which a death is brought about and offered. That's why for example, altars are not found in many non-Catholic churches; most non-Catholics do not believe that they are offering a sacrificial Victim to God. Incidentally, Catholics often speak about receiving the "Host" at Mass. The Latin for victim is "Host" (*hostia*). In saying that we receive the Host in Holy Communion we mean that we consume Jesus, who is our Sacrificial Victim—the Lamb of God. There on the altar, Jesus gives Himself to us as the Perfect Victim whose obedience is offered to God the Father to counterbalance our sins.

Are We Killing Jesus At The Mass?

It must be stressed that at Mass, we are NOT killing Jesus. Rather, what's happening is, Jesus' two thousand year old Sacrifice is mystically *made present*...transported through time and space, as it were. And since it is not a new sacrifice, it is not a new suffering. Rather, Jesus' two thousand year old suffering is *made present* on the altar.

Offering Our Lives Alongside Jesus'

When we go to Mass we would do well to remember that we are actually attending the Crucifixion of Jesus and should intentionally join with the priest in offering Jesus' Perfect loving obedience to God the Father. But in addition to Christ's Sacrifice, we should offer God *our own* good deeds and sacrifices performed throughout the week. On their own, our good deeds have little merit, but when offered alongside the Sacrifice of Jesus, our good deeds become so much more pleasing and acceptable to God.

Through The Mass We Give God His Due

Each and every day all around the globe (except for Good Friday) the perfect obedience of Jesus is offered to God the Father as a satisfaction for the sins of the whole world. And yet the "whole world" cannot claim to be in a just relationship with God simply because a Mass was offered. It is only through being united to Jesus in His death, burial and resurrection (through baptism) that an individual can appropriate God's forgiveness and dare to claim His obedience and justice as their own (Phil 3:8-9).

PRAYER

Dear Lord, it is amazing and wonderful to consider what really happens at Mass. Help me to be mindful that when I go to Mass, I am really attending your Sacrifice. Help me to join with the priest in offering your obedience to make up for the sins I may have committed during the week. I look forward to offering my own good deeds to you, alongside your Perfect Sacrifice. I ask that my reverence for the Eucharist be deepened and that you would bless me with a humble and grateful spirit so that I might receive you in a worthy manner. Each time Mass is offered, you make up for my sins and unite me to you! This is an incomprehensible truth. May I grow in love of the Mass more and more until the day you call me to be with you in heaven. Amen!

Questions:

1. T/F Jesus' Sacrifice had the power to make up for all sins, past, present and future.
2. T/F Jesus' Sacrifice was immediately applied to counterbalance all sins, past present and future.
3. How do we fully make up for our sins today...what can we offer to God to make up for them?
4. Besides Jesus' Sacrifice, what else should we offer to God the Father at the Mass?
5. What would you say to someone who claimed that Jesus was being made to suffer at the Mass?
6. Explain how the priest dramatizes Jesus' death at the Mass.
7. What does the word "Host" mean?

ABBREVIATIONS

CCC   *The Catechism of The Catholic Church*

DS   *Heinrich Denzinger: The Sources of Catholic Dogma*

NIV   *New International Version*

LG   *Lumen Gentium*

ABOUT THE AUTHOR

Damien Connolly is an Irish native. He received his undergraduate degree in Theology and Philosophy from the University of Limerick and later received his Master's in Theology from Holy Apostles College and Seminary in Cromwell, CT. He has been teaching Theology at the college preparatory level since 2003. From an early age, Connolly began seeking the answers to life's fundamental questions and hopes this publication will serve others on their quest to better understand the Crucifixion of Jesus. He is also the author of **Exploring the Twenty Mysteries of the Holy Rosary** and **The Irish Accordion Tutor, Vol 1.**

damienjconnolly@hotmail.com

Made in the USA
Middletown, DE
28 November 2018